Theme Skills Tests
Table of Contents

Name_____

Practice Test

Hen Went Fast

I make the cake.

I make the cake fast!

I make the hats.

I make the hats fast!

Wake up Hen!
Wake up FAST!

1. **What does Hen make for her friends to wear?**

   ○ cake
   ○ wake
   ○ hats

2. **What does Hen do at the end of the story?**

○   ○   ○

All Together Now
Level 1, Theme 1
Theme Skills Test Record

Student _____ Date _____

Student Record Form

	Possible Score	Criterion Score	Student Score
Part A: Consonants *m*, *s*, *c*, *t*; Blending Short *a* Words	5	4	
Part B: Consonants *n*, *f*, *p*; Blending Short *a* Words	5	4	
Part C: Consonants *b*, *r*, *h*, *g*; Blending Short *i* Words	5	4	
Part D: High-Frequency Words	5	4	
Part E: Sequence of Events	5	4	
Part F: Compare and Contrast	5	4	
Part G: Cause and Effect	5	4	
TOTAL	35	28	

Total Student Score x 2.86 = _____ %

Name_____

Consonants *m*, *s*, *c*, *t*; Blending Short *a* Words

1.

s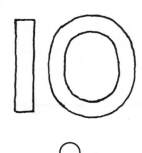

○   ○   ○

2.

m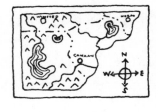

○   ○   ○

3.

t

○   ○   ○

 **Go on**

4.

C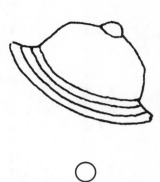

○   ○   ○

5.

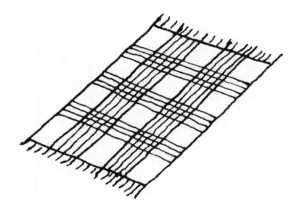

○ **cat**

○ **Sam**

○ **mat**

Consonants *n*, *f*, *p*; Blending Short *a* Words

1.

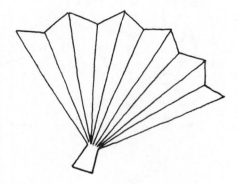

○ **fat**

○ **fan**

○ **tan**

2.

○ **mat**

○ **pan**

○ **man**

3.

○ **cap**

○ **cat**

○ **Nan**

Go on →

4.

    ○ tap

    ○ pan

    ○ fan

5.

    ○ Nan

    ○ Sam

    ○ nap

C Name_____

Consonants *b*, *r*, *h*, *g*; Blending Short *i* Words

1. Duck picked up his  .

- ○ tip
- ○ bat
- ○ bit

2. He put a helmet over his 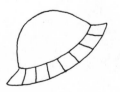 .

- ○ hit
- ○ rip
- ○ hat

Go on

3. Duck wanted to get a big  .

- ○ hit
- ○ pin
- ○ hip

4.  threw the ball, and Duck took a swing.

- ○ Big
- ○ Tip
- ○ Pig

5. Duck hit the ball and fast.

- ○ ran
- ○ fit
- ○ map

D Name_____

High-Frequency Words

1. Nan can _____.

   ○ to
   ○ jump
   ○ have

2. We can jump, _____.

   ○ one
   ○ too
   ○ go

3. Nat can _____ jump.

   ○ on
   ○ who
   ○ not

4. We can _____ a big one here.

   ○ find
   ○ go
   ○ the

5. We can jump _____ jump!

   ○ here
   ○ find
   ○ and

E Name_____

Sequence of Events

Who Can Sit?

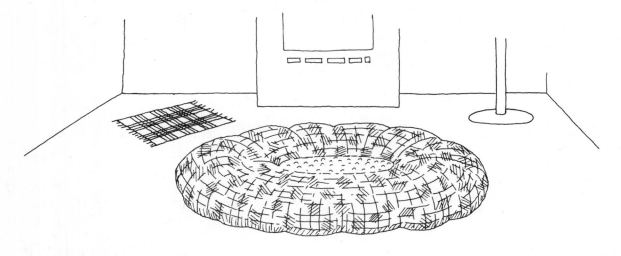

Tim Cat can sit.

Nat and Nan can sit.

Go on

Pat can sit, too.

Big Cat can not sit.
It can not fit!

Go find a mat, Big Cat.
Sit on the mat, Big Cat.

Go on

1. Who sits on the pillow first?

○   ○   ○

Nan   **Tim Cat**   **Big Cat**

2. Who comes and sits down next?

○   ○   ○

Nat and Nan   **Nan and Big Cat**   **Nat and Pat**

3. Then who comes and sits down?

- ○ Nan and Nat
- ○ Tim Cat
- ○ Pat

4. Who comes along last and can't fit?

- ○ Nat and Pat
- ○ Big Cat
- ○ Pat

5. Then what does Pat tell Big Cat to do?

- ○ sit on Nan
- ○ jump on Tim Cat
- ○ sit on a mat

Name_____

Compare and Contrast

A Cat and a Pig

Pam and Tan have a big pig.

Pam and Tan have a big, fat pig.

A pig can not jump.

It can sit, sit, sit.

Pat and Nat have a big cat.

Pat and Nat have a big, big cat.

A cat can jump.

It can sit, too.

1. Pam and Tan have a pet _____ .

○ cat

○ pig

○ Pat

2. Pat and Nat have a pet _____ .

○ cat

○ pig

○ rat

3. Both pets are _____ .

○ big

○ tan

○ fat

4. The cat can _____. The pig can't.

- ○ sip
- ○ sit
- ○ jump

5. Both pets can _____.

- ○ jump
- ○ sit
- ○ bat

G Name_____

Cause and Effect

Who Ran?

A big cat ran.

Tip ran.

The man ran, too.

The cat ran.

Tip sat.

Go on ➡

Tip sat, sat, sat.

The man sat, too.
Here, Tip.
We can sit a bit.

1. The dog ran away because

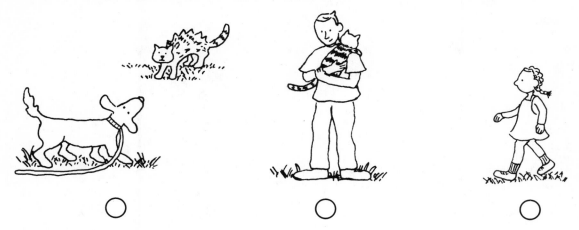

○　　　　　　　○　　　　　　　○

2. The cat ran because

○　　　　　　　○　　　　　　　○

Go on ⇨

3. **The dog sat because**

 ○    ○    ○

4. **The man was tired, so**

 ○    ○    ○

5. **The man and dog went away, so**

 ○    ○    ○

STOP

Surprise!
Level 1, Theme 2
Theme Skills Test Record

Student _____ Date _____

Student Record Form	Possible Score	Criterion Score	Student Score
Part A: Consonants *d*, *w*, *l*, *x*; Blending Short *o* Words	5	4	
Part B: Consonants *y*, *k*, *v*; Blending Short *e* Words	5	4	
Part C: Consonants *q*, *j*, *z*; Blending Short *u* Words	5	4	
Part D: High-Frequency Words	5	4	
Part E: Noting Details	5	4	
Part F: Fantasy and Realism	5	4	
Part G: Story Structure	5	4	
TOTAL	35	28	
	Total Student Score x 2.86 =		%

Consonants *d, w, l, x;* Blending Short *o* Words

1.

d

○   ○   ○

2.

w

○   ○   ○

3.

l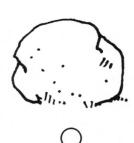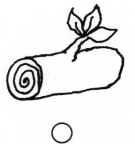

○   ○   ○

4.

○ fox

○ fin

○ fix

5.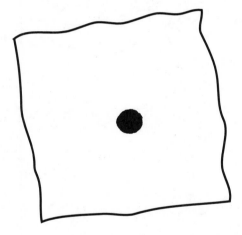

○ top

○ dig

○ dot

STOP

Consonants *y, k, v;* Blending Short *e* Words

1. Marcy's _____ is sick.

   ○ den
   ○ pot
   ○ pet

2. Marcy and her mom _____ into the van.

   ○ get
   ○ bed
   ○ got

Go on

3. They take the pup to see the _____.

- ○ web
- ○ yet
- ○ vet

4. The vet takes medicine from her _____.

- ○ kit
- ○ fed
- ○ hen

5. Marcy's pup will take more medicine for _____ days.

- ○ yet
- ○ ten
- ○ Ken

Consonants *q*, *j*, *z*; Blending Short *u* Words

1.

j
 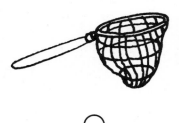 

○ ○ ○

2.

z

○ ○ ○

3.

qu
 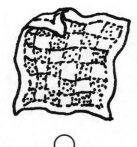 

○ ○ ○

4.

○ **nut**

○ **tub**

○ **net**

5.

○ **mud**

○ **jet**

○ **jug**

High-Frequency Words

1. "You can not find me," _____ Ben.

- ○ does
- ○ said
- ○ pull

2. "Go!" said Jan. "I can find _____ ."

- ○ do
- ○ you
- ○ me

Go on ⟶

3. "One, two, _____ , four, five," said Jan.

- ○ they
- ○ once
- ○ three

4. Jan said, "Ben, _____ are you?"

- ○ where
- ○ what
- ○ away

5. "You _____ in here!" said Jan.

- ○ my
- ○ for
- ○ are

Noting Details

Dan and Pug

Pug dug.

Pug dug, dug, dug.

"It is hot, hot, hot," said Dan.

"Are you too hot, Pug?"

Dan got a big, big box for Pug.

"Here is a box," said Dan.

"You can sit here."

Go on

Dan cut the big box.

Dan cut, cut, cut.

He got a tan rug for the box.

Dan set it in the pen.

"Go on in, Pug," said Dan.

"You can sit, sit, sit.

It is not hot, hot, hot."

1. **What kind of day was it?**

   ○ wet

   ○ not hot

   ○ hot

2. **What did Pug do at the beginning of the story?**

   ○ Pug dug and dug.

   ○ Pug ran and ran.

   ○ Pug got wet.

Go on ⟹

3. What did Dan use to make a shady place for Pug?

   ○ a bus
   ○ a bun
   ○ a box

4. What did Dan put into the box for Pug?

   ○ a rag
   ○ a rug
   ○ a rub

5. Where did Dan put the box after he fixed it up?

   ○ in a big red van
   ○ in a big lot
   ○ in the pen for Pug

Fantasy and Realism

The Box

Ben dug in a big box.

He got a wig for Sox Cat.

"The wig is a hit!" said Kit Fox.

"Get me a wig, Ben!"

Go on

"Got it!" said Ben.

"My wig!" said Kit Fox.

"I can do a jig in my wig," said Kit Fox.
"You can jig, too."

"I can jig," said Sox Cat.
"But it is hot in here!"

Go on

Ben got a fan for Sox Cat.

"The fan is a hit!" said Kit Fox.
"Get me a fan, Ben!"

"Got it!" said Ben.
"Sit, Kit Fox!
You can not jig and fan too."

"I can," said Kit Fox.
"I can fan and jig, jig and fan!"

Go on →

1. Which can not be real?

    ○   ○   ○

2. Which can not be real?

    ○   ○   ○

Go on

3. Which can be real?

      ○   ○   ○

4. What can a real cat do?

  ○ live in a pot

  ○ do a jig

  ○ jump on a cot

5. Which can be real?

  ○ "The wig is a hit!" said Kit Fox.

  ○ Ben dug in the big box.

  ○ "I can jig," said Sox Cat.

Name_____

Story Structure

A Hug for Zig

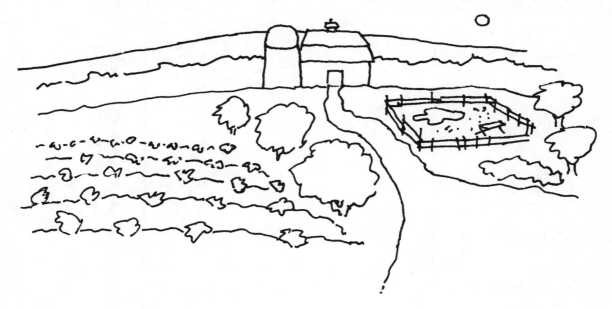

Zig is a big pig.
Jen and Zig live here.

Once Jen got a big hat.
Jen said, "My hat is big.
It is too big!
What can I do, Zig?"

"Get a big wig," said Zig.

Jen got a wig.

Jen got a big, big wig.

Go on →

"Does the hat fit?" said

"It does fit!" said Jen.
"My hat is not big.
But you get a big,
big hug."

1. Where does this story take place?

   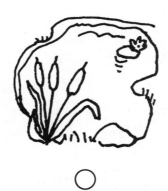   

◯   ◯   ◯

2. Who is in this story?

○   ○   ○

3. What is Jen's problem?

○ The hat is too big.
○ The pig is too fat.
○ The pen is too wet.

4. What does Zig tell Jen to do?

○ Cut the hat in two.
○ Get the hat wet.
○ Get a big wig.

5. How does the story end?

○ Zig gets a big, big hug.
○ Zig gets a bat.
○ Zig gets a hat, too.

Let's Look Around!
Level 1, Theme 3
Theme Skills Test Record

Student _____ Date _____

Student Record Form

	Possible Score	Criterion Score	Student Score
Part A: Blending More Short *a* Words	5	4	
Part B: Blending More Short *i* Words	5	4	
Part C: Double Final Consonants	5	4	
Part D: Plurals with -*s*; Verb Endings -*s*, -*ed*, -*ing*	5	4	
Part E: Clusters with *r*	5	4	
Part F: Possessives with '*s*; Contractions with '*s*	5	4	
Part G: High-Frequency Words	5	4	
Part H: Topic, Main Idea, Details/Summarizing	5	4	
Part I: Making Predictions	5	4	
Part J: Categorize and Classify	5	4	
Part K: Spelling	5	4	
Part L: Grammar	5	4	
TOTAL 60	48		

Total Student Score x 1.67 = _____ %

Blending More Short *a* Words

1. Nat sat on Pam's _____.

○ lip
○ pass
○ lap

2. Pam had a _____ for Nat.

○ map
○ wax
○ mop

Go on ⟹

3. "Can you find the _____?" said Pam.

- ○ bass
- ○ big
- ○ bag

4. Nat _____ to find the bag.

- ○ rack
- ○ ran
- ○ rug

5. "_____ got it for you!" said Pam.

- ○ Did
- ○ Back
- ○ Dad

Blending More Short *i* Words

1. Is my cat _____?

   ○ sack
   ○ sick
   ○ sock

2. We will get _____ to the vet.

   ○ him
   ○ miss
   ○ ham

3. The vet pats _____ back.

- ○ has
- ○ his
- ○ lick

4. The vet has a _____ for my cat.

- ○ pal
- ○ pass
- ○ pill

5. Look! My cat is not sick! The vet _____ it!

- ○ dips
- ○ did
- ○ dad

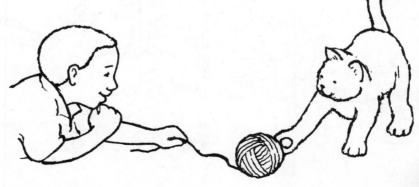

Name_____

Double Final Consonants

1. Ben and I will go on a trip. We _____ one brown bag.

○ tack

○ pack

○ pull

2. We _____ the van.

○ fill

○ kiss

○ five

3. We _____ a big bag to Rick.

- ○ pill
- ○ fall
- ○ pass

4. We sit in the _____ of the van.

- ○ back
- ○ bill
- ○ bass

5. Dad will _____ Ben and me!

- ○ hill
- ○ miss
- ○ mill

D Name_____

Plurals with *-s*; Verb Endings *-s*, *-ed*, *-ing*

1. Dan has three _____.

   ○ cat
   ○ sat
   ○ cats

2. Dan is _____ for his pets.

   ○ looks
   ○ looking
   ○ looked

3. Dan _____ Fan and Tan.

- ○ finding
- ○ finds
- ○ find

4. "Van! Van!" _____ Dan. "Where are you?"

- ○ calls
- ○ calling
- ○ call

5. "Here you are, Van! I _____ it for you."

- ○ filled
- ○ filling
- ○ fill

Clusters with *r*

1. Pug is my pet. Pug can

   do a _____.

   ○ trick

   ○ brick

   ○ tick

2. Pug likes to dig in the _____.

   ○ brass

   ○ grass

   ○ gas

Go on ⇒

3. Pug likes to go on _____.

- ○ grips
- ○ trips
- ○ rips

4. Pug sees a bug in a _____.

- ○ rack
- ○ track
- ○ crack

5. If Pug gets wet, he _____!

- ○ dips
- ○ grins
- ○ drips

Possessives with 's; Contractions with 's

1. Jan said, "_____ look for my hat!"

   ○ It's
   ○ Let's
   ○ He's

2. "_____ hat is not here," said Tim.

   ○ Jan's
   ○ Jan
   ○ Jigs

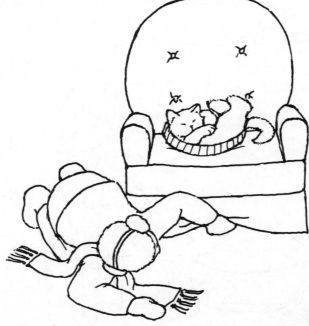

3. "And _____ not here," said Ken.

- ○ let's
- ○ it
- ○ it's

4. "_____ my hat!" said Jan. "Mitt has it."

- ○ He's
- ○ Who's
- ○ Here's

5. "_____ a cat on a hat!" said Tim.

- ○ He's
- ○ Let's
- ○ He

Name_____

High-Frequency Words

1. It is fall, but it is not too _____ yet.

   ○ eat
   ○ call
   ○ cold

2. What can I see in the fall? I see

   a _____.

   ○ blue
   ○ bird
   ○ funny

Go on ➡

3. I see a fall _____.

- ○ full
- ○ flower
- ○ first

4. Look! Here is an _____. It has some nuts.

- ○ all
- ○ animal
- ○ also

5. I _____ fall!

- ○ like
- ○ look
- ○ shall

Topic, Main Idea, Details/Summarizing

Some pets are cats.
Cats like to nap.
Cats nap, nap, nap.
Cats like to sit and lick.
Cats lick, lick, lick.
Some cats can do tricks.
My cats can!

I like cats a lot!
You can hug a cat.
You can pat a cat.
A cat will lick you.
A cat will sit on a lap.
A cat is a pal!
As I said, I like cats, cats, cats!

1. Which words best tell what the story is mostly about?

   ○ all pets
   ○ a girl
   ○ pet cats

2. What is one thing the storyteller says that cats like to do?

   ○ nap
   ○ drip
   ○ hiss

3. What is one thing the storyteller can do with a cat?

   ○ mix it
   ○ hug it
   ○ grab it

4. Which one sentence best tells what the girl thinks about cats?

- ○ The girl likes cats to nap.
- ○ The girl likes what cats do.
- ○ The girl does not like cats.

5. What is the best title for this selection?

- ○ Tricks a Cat Can Do
- ○ Pat, the Cat
- ○ Why I Like Cats

I Name_____

Making Predictions

Dad will cut some flowers.

1. **Which picture shows what Dad might ask Sam to help him do?**

  ○   ○   ○

Go on ⟹

"Look at the big red flowers," said Pat.
"Can you cut some, Dad?"

"I can," said Dad.
"I can cut, cut, cut."

**2. What do you think Dad will
do next?**

   ○ **cut the green grass**
   ○ **get rid of the flowers**
   ○ **cut some red flowers**

Pat said, "Do not cut all the big red flowers, Dad.
But you can trim the grass. Trim it, Dad."

3. What do you think Dad will do next?

   ○ **cut the grass**
   ○ **color the grass green**
   ○ **cut some flowers for the birds**

"Can you get a jug, Sam?" said Dad.

"Get the big tan jug. It is in the den, Sam."

4. What do you think Sam will do?

- ○ go and get the tan jug
- ○ go and get a big box
- ○ go and sit in the grass

"I did get a jug. I got the big tan jug," said Sam.

"The tan jug will not do, Sam!" said Dad.

"It has a big, big crack in it."

"Here is a big pot," said Pat.

"It is not cracked. It will do!"

5. **Which picture shows what Dad will do with the flowers?**

○   ○   ○

Categorize and Classify

I live in a big pack.

I can get in a den.

I nap in a den.

What kind of animal am I?

I live where it is wet.

I have fins.

I can fit in cracks.

What kind of animal am I?

I quack, quack, quack.

I drip, drip, drip.

I like it where it is wet.

I have a bill, but not fins.

What kind of animal am I?

I can trot, trot, trot.

I trot in the grass.

I can eat grass.

What kind of animal am I?

I am a big, big, cat.

I like to nap in the grass.

Do not pat a big, big, cat!

1. Which kind of animal lives in a pack?

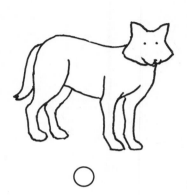  

○   ○   ○

2. Which kind of animal lives in the water?

○   ○   ○

Go on

3. Which kind of animal is a big cat?

       ○   ○   ○

4. Which kind of animal has a bill but no fins?

       ○   ○   ○

5. What is a good title for this selection?

   ○ **Let's Go to the Vet**

   ○ **Let's Look at Animals**

   ○ **Let's Plan a Trip**

Spelling

1. **Dick and I are going on a _____.**

- ○ tirp
- ○ trip
- ○ tripp

2. **We _____ in the back.**

- ○ sitt
- ○ ist
- ○ sit

3. We see a _____.

○ na

○ mann

○ man

4. He has a _____ on his lap!

○ cat

○ catt

○ ta

5. His pet is _____!

○ gib

○ big

○ bigg

L Name_____

Grammar

1. Which one of these is a sentence?

- ○ Pat and Tim
- ○ Pat and Tim sit here.
- ○ sit here

2. Which one of these is not a sentence?

- ○ at a big bug
- ○ They look at a bug.
- ○ They like the bug.

3. What is the naming part of this sentence?

Pat looks at the bug.

- ○ looks at
- ○ the bug
- ○ Pat

4. What is the action part of this sentence?

The cat jumps at the bug.

- ○ jumps
- ○ cat
- ○ at the bug

5. What is the naming part of this sentence?

The bug gets away!

- ○ gets
- ○ away
- ○ bug

Family and Friends
Level 1, Theme 4
Theme Skills Test Record

Student _____   Date _____

Student Record Form

	Possible Score	Criterion Score	Student Score
Part A: Blending More Short *o* Words	10	8	
Part B: Blending More Short *e* Words	10	8	
Part C: Blending More Short *u* Words	10	8	
Part D: Clusters with *l*, with *s*, Triple Clusters	10	8	
Part E: High-Frequency Words	5	4	
Part F: Drawing Conclusions	5	4	
Part G: Compare and Contrast	5	4	
Part H: Sequence of Events	5	4	
Part I: Spelling	5	4	
Part J: Grammar	5	4	
TOTAL	70	56	

Total Student Score x 1.43 = _____ %

Name_____

Blending More Short *o* Words

1.

   sack   sock   sick

   ○   ○   ○

2.

   rack   crack   rock

   ○   ○   ○

3.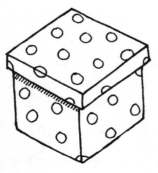

   box   bricks   backs

   ○   ○   ○

Go on →

4.

map   mop   mess

◯   ◯   ◯

5.

doll   dill   drop

◯   ◯   ◯

6.

pet   trap   pot

◯   ◯   ◯

7.

trick   block   black

◯   ◯   ◯

Go on →

8.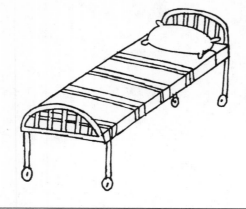

tock   cot   cab

◯   ◯   ◯

9.

clock   click   clack

◯   ◯   ◯

10.

lag   gill   log

◯   ◯   ◯

STOP

Blending More Short *e* Words

1.

bad   bid   bed

○   ○   ○

2.

well   will   wag

○   ○   ○

3.

pin   plan   pen

○   ○   ○

Go on ⟩

4.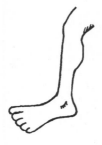

glad ○   leg ○   log ○

5.

jot ○   jam ○   jet ○

6.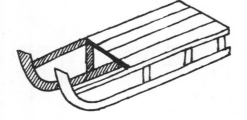

sled ○   slit ○   lads ○

7.

step ○   stop ○   stem ○

 Go on →

8.

dress   desk   dock

◯   ◯   ◯

9.

egg   leg   get

◯   ◯   ◯

10.

stack   neck   nest

◯   ◯   ◯

STOP

Name_____

Blending More Short *u* Words

1.

dock   duck   deck

○   ○   ○

2.

jug   jig   jog

○   ○   ○

3.

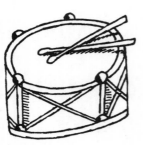

rim   drop   drum

○   ○   ○

Go on

4.

sum ○   sad ○   sun ○

5.

bass ○   bus ○   bit ○

6.

cut ○   tack ○   cot ○

7.

pop ○   pit ○   pup ○

Go on ▷

8.

pack   cup   cap

◯   ◯   ◯

9.

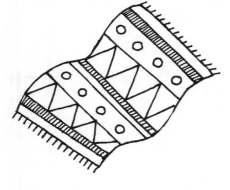

rig   drag   rug

◯   ◯   ◯

10.

cub   cob   cabs

◯   ◯   ◯

STOP

D Name_____

Clusters with *l*, with *s*, Triple Clusters

1.

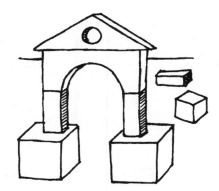

    clocks   blocks   flocks

      ◯   ◯   ◯

2.

    slam   ham   clam

    ◯   ◯   ◯

3.

    flag   lag   glad

    ◯   ◯   ◯

Go on ⇨

4.

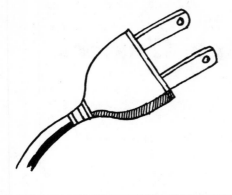

slug   plug   snug
○   ○   ○

5.

scrap   class   glass
○   ○   ○

6.

smock   sock   mock
○   ○   ○

7.

kicks   sick   stick
○   ○   ○

Go on →

8.

skip   sip   flip

○   ○   ○

9.

cub   scrub   rub

○   ○   ○

10.

trap   strap   sap

○   ○   ○

High-Frequency Words

1. "Let's do some spelling _____ ," said
   Mr. Cox.

   ○ their
   ○ today
   ○ read

2. "Did you _____ to spell <u>vest</u>?" asked
   Mr. Cox.

   ○ learn
   ○ love
   ○ walk

Go on ➡

3. "I did!" said Fran. "I can _____ vest, too."

- ○ your
- ○ would
- ○ write

4. The _____ looked to see Fran write.

- ○ children
- ○ car
- ○ come

5. "Look at the _____ ," said Mr. Cox. "Who can spell drum?"

- ○ people
- ○ picture
- ○ play

Drawing Conclusions

For Dad

Sam said, "I got Dad a brass box.
It has a lock in it. What did you get
Dad, Rick?"

Rick said, "I got Dad a black hat.
It will fit him. What did you pick
for Dad, Nan?"

"I did not pick yet!" said Nan.

"You did not pick yet!" yelled Sam and Rick.

"I did not pick!" yelled Nan. "What can I get Dad?"

1. Whose birthday do you think it is?

- ○ Nan's
- ○ Rick's
- ○ Dad's

2. Who hasn't bought a gift yet?

- ○ Rick
- ○ Nan
- ○ Sam

"Here is a plan," said Rick.
"You can write a list for Dad."

"A list?" asked Nan.

"Yes," said Rick. "Get some
paper, Nan."

3. **What will Rick help Nan do?**

    ○ color a picture for Dad
    ○ write what Nan will do for Dad
    ○ get a pup for Dad

4. **Besides some paper, what else does
    Nan need?**

    ○ a pen
    ○ a hat
    ○ some tacks

Here is Nan's list.

> Dad,
>   I will get the paper for you.
>   I will walk Spot.
>   I will fix ham and eggs for you.
>   You will get a big, big hug
> and a big, big kiss.
>   Love,
>   Nan

5. How do you think Dad will feel about Nan's gift?

○ **It will make him sad.**

○ **He will not like it.**

○ **He will love it.**

STOP

Compare and Contrast

Ruff's Family

I am Jeff.

I am ten.

I run.

Ruff is my dog.

Ruff is six.

Ruff runs.

Mom runs, too.

Mom runs at the track.

Ruff runs at the track.

Go on ➡

Dad walks.

Dad does not run.

Ruff walks.

Ruff stops and smells the flowers.

Jill sits and reads.

Ruff sits on Jill's lap.

But Ruff does not read!

Go on ⇨

1. How are all the people in this story alike?

   ○ They all run.
   ○ They all like Ruff.
   ○ They all just sit and sit.

2. Who in this family runs?

   ○ Jeff, Mom, and Jill
   ○ Jill, Jeff, and Dad
   ○ Ruff, Jeff, and Mom

3. What does Jill do that is different from the other people in her family?

   ○ Jill sits and reads.
   ○ Jill runs with Dad.
   ○ Jill runs at the track.

4. How are Jeff and Jill alike?

   ○ Jeff and Jill do not read.
   ○ Jeff and Jill are six.
   ○ Jeff and Jill are children.

5. How is Jeff different from Dad?

   ○ Jeff has a pet, but Dad does not.
   ○ Jeff runs, but Dad walks.
   ○ Jeff likes flowers, but Dad does not.

Let's Cut Flowers

"Look at the flowers!" said Kim.

"Can I cut flowers, Miss Brill?" asked Ann.

"Can I cut, too?" asked Kim.

"Yes," said Miss Brill.

"First, get red, blue, and green paper."

"Next, cut stems," said Miss Brill.
"Cut lots of stems."

"Next, cut flowers,"
said Miss Brill. "Cut, cut, cut!"

"Red is best," said Kim.

"Yes, red is best," said Ann.

"Can I pin up the stems, Miss Brill?" Kim asked.
"Yes," said Miss Brill.
"Ann will pin flowers on top
of the stems."

Go on

"Can I cut a flower?" asked Bill.

"Can I cut a flower?" asked Ted.

"Yes," said Miss Brill.
"Cut, cut, cut!"

1. **Where did the girls get the idea for the garden?**

      ◯   ◯   ◯

2. **What did Miss Brill tell the girls to do first?**

    ◯ cut the flowers

    ◯ pin the flowers on the stems

    ◯ get red, blue, and green paper

3. What part of the plants did the girls cut out last?

○ the stems
○ the flowers
○ the pins

4. What part of the plants did Kim pin up first?

○ the brown sticks
○ the flowers
○ the green stems

5. What happened last in the story?

○ Bill and Ted asked to cut flowers.
○ The children did not like the flowers.
○ Bill and Ted picked the flowers.

Name_____

Spelling

1. **Bud and I have** _____.

    ○ **funn**

    ○ **fen**

    ○ **fun**

2. **We like to** _____.

    ○ **runn**

    ○ **run**

    ○ **rune**

3. We go _____ the big hill.

- ○ upp
- ○ upu
- ○ up

4. We do _____ stop!

- ○ nte
- ○ nott
- ○ not

5. We _____ to the top fast.

- ○ get
- ○ gget
- ○ gat

Name_____

Grammar

1. Which one of these is an asking sentence?

○ Is your pet a cat?

○ I call my cat Fluff.

○ Fluff sits and licks.

2. Which one of these is an asking sentence?

○ The frog is green.

○ The cat bats at the frog.

○ Does the cat like to play?

Go on

3. Which one of these is a telling sentence?

○ Is a pig a pet?
○ My friend has a pet pig.
○ What does she call the pig?

4. Which one of these is a telling sentence?

○ Did the big pig win?
○ Can the pig do a trick?
○ The big pig did win.

5. Which one of these is not a sentence?

○ spins and spins
○ What is the animal doing?
○ The animal spins a web.

STOP

Home Sweet Home
Level 1, Theme 5
Theme Skills Test Record

Student _____   Date _____

Student Record Form

	Possible Score	Criterion Score	Student Score
Part A: Digraphs *sh, th, wh, ch, tch*	10	8	
Part B: Long *a* (CVC*e*)	10	8	
Part C: Long *i* (CVC*e*)	10	8	
Part D: Final *nd, nk, ng*	10	8	
Part E: Contractions	10	8	
Part F: High-Frequency Words	5	4	
Part G: Compare and Contrast	5	4	
Part H: Making Generalizations	5	4	
Part I: Cause and Effect	5	4	
Part J: Spelling	5	4	
Part K: Grammar	5	4	
Part L: Writing Skills	5	4	
TOTAL	85	68	
		Total Student Score x 1.18 =	%

Digraphs *sh*, *th*, *wh*, *ch*, *tch*

Read each sentence. Then fill in the circle next to the word that makes sense in the sentence.

1. I got my cat, Mitts, at a pet _____.

   ○ shop
   ○ chop
   ○ hop

2. I fill a _____ for Mitts.

   ○ drink
   ○ ditch
   ○ dish

3. Mitts is _____, but she will grow.

- ○ thin
- ○ chin
- ○ shin

4. I like to sit _____ Mitts.

- ○ whiff
- ○ with
- ○ wit

5. _____ I nap, Mitts naps too.

- ○ When
- ○ Hen
- ○ Them

Go on ⟹

6. Once Mitts got up, but I did not get

up _____.

- ○ ten
- ○ hen
- ○ then

7. Mitts just had to do a big _____.

- ○ such
- ○ stretch
- ○ rush

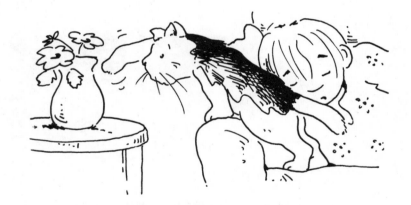

8. All at once, I could hear a _____.

- ○ crash
- ○ catch
- ○ chap

Go on ⟹

9. "Mitts!" I said. "The vase has a big
_____ in it!"

- ○ ship
- ○ chip
- ○ hip

10. But I still like Mitts so _____.

- ○ much
- ○ mush
- ○ chum

Long *a* (CVC*e*)

Read each sentence. Then fill in the circle next to the word that makes sense in the sentence.

1. "Let's bake a _____!" said Mom.

    ○ crack
    ○ cake
    ○ cast

2. Jake said, "I never _____ a cake."

    ○ mill
    ○ mad
    ○ made

Go on ⇨

3. Mom said, "_____ these for me, Jake."

○ Tack
○ Take
○ Sink

4. "What _____ shall we make it?" asked Mom.

○ shape
○ ship
○ shop

5. "That one," said Jake. "Then we can make a _____ on it."

○ fast
○ fat
○ face

Go on

6. "I can _____ a big grin on this face,"
said Jake.

○ make

○ mask

○ mink

7. "First we have to _____ the cake,"
said Mom.

○ blink

○ bake

○ back

8. "Let's find a _____ for the cake," said
Mom.

○ late

○ last

○ plate

Go on ➡

9. "Let's write Dad's _____ on it!" said Jake.

- ○ man
- ○ name
- ○ nap

10. Just then, Dad _____ into the room.

- ○ came
- ○ camp
- ○ can

STOP

Long *i* (CVC*e*)

Read each sentence. Then fill in the circle next to the word that makes sense in the sentence.

1. "_____ to get up, Jan!" said Dad.

   ○ Tame
   ○ Time
   ○ Tim

2. "What a _____ day!" said Dad.

   ○ fine
   ○ fame
   ○ fin

Go on ⟶

3. "It's _____!" said Dad. "Time to get up!"

○ nine
○ name
○ knit

4. "Let's go!" said Dad. "You can not _____ in that bed."

○ hid
○ hand
○ hide

5. "What would you _____ to do today?" Dad asked.

○ lake
○ like
○ lick

6. "I would like to _____ bikes," said Jan.

   ○ ride
   ○ rid
   ○ grade

7. "Then I would like to go for a _____,"
   she added.

   ○ hit
   ○ hike
   ○ hank

8. "Let's _____ two miles to the lake,"
   said Dad.

   ○ daze
   ○ drag
   ○ drive

Go on →

9. "Can I take my _____?" asked Jan.

- ○ kite
- ○ kit
- ○ gate

10. "We will have a _____ time," Dad said to Jan.

- ○ nick
- ○ nice
- ○ name

STOP

Final *nd*, *nk*, *ng*

Say the picture name. Then read the words. Fill in the circle below the word that names the picture.

1.

     king   kit   kid
     ◯   ◯   ◯

2.

     band   bang   bank
     ◯   ◯   ◯

3.

     rink   ring   rig
     ◯   ◯   ◯

4.

sink ○   skin ○   skunk ○

5.

wing ○   win ○   wink ○

6.

brand ○   truck ○   trunk ○

7.

thank ○   tank ○   tack ○

Go on

8.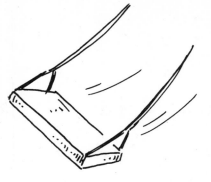

     sank   swing   sing

     ◯   ◯   ◯

9.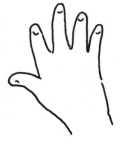

     had   hunk   hand

     ◯   ◯   ◯

10.

     band   bank   bad

     ◯   ◯   ◯

STOP

E   Name_____

Contractions

Read each sentence. Look at the underlined words. Fill in the circle next to the short way to write these words.

1. Dave was going to fly his kite. "<u>Let us</u> go!" he called to Pat.

   ○ We'll

   ○ Let's

   ○ Vet's

2. Pat said, "This <u>is not</u> a good day for kites."

   ○ isn't

   ○ wasn't

   ○ it's

3. "Why not?" asked Dave. "<u>We will</u> have fun!"
he added.

- ○ We'd
- ○ We'll
- ○ We've

4. "I <u>do not</u> see much wind today," said Pat.

- ○ won't
- ○ didn't
- ○ don't

5. "I think <u>we would</u> find wind at the lake,"
said Dave.

- ○ you'd
- ○ we'll
- ○ we'd

6. "<u>You are</u> doing a good job, Dave," said Pat.

○ You've

○ You're

○ You'll

7. "<u>I have</u> never had such a good time!" said Dave.

○ I've

○ We've

○ I'd

Go on

8. "<u>Would not</u> you like to fly my kite?" asked Dave.

   ○ Won't
   ○ Can't
   ○ Wouldn't

9. "<u>I would</u> like to fly it," said Pat. "Let me have it."

   ○ I'd
   ○ I'll
   ○ We'll

10. "You <u>will not</u> let it get away, will you?" asked Dave.

    ○ wouldn't
    ○ won't
    ○ we'd

Name_____

High-Frequency Words

Read each sentence. Then fill in the circle next to the word that makes sense in the sentence.

1. This is the _____ where my family lives.

   ◯ how
   ◯ house
   ◯ these

2. _____ house is made of brick.

   ◯ Own
   ◯ Over
   ◯ Our

3. Our house is _____, but I like it.

- ○ world
- ○ little
- ○ light

4. It's nice that I have my own _____.

- ○ room
- ○ right
- ○ good

5. Do you see the box where I _____ flowers?

- ○ give
- ○ more
- ○ grow

G Name_____

Compare and Contrast

Read each part of the story. Then read each question. Fill in the circle next to the best answer.

Who Does What?

At nine, all three children wake up.

Beth and Mike make their beds.

But Sam will not make his bed.

Sam is playing with his truck.

1. **What do Beth, Mike, and Sam all do?**

   ○ play with their trucks
   ○ make their beds
   ○ wake up

2. What does Sam do that Beth and Mike do not do?

○ stays in bed
○ plays with his truck
○ makes his bed

3. How are Beth and Mike alike?

○ They don't wake up on time.
○ They bake a cake.
○ They make their beds.

Go on

Beth, Mike, and Sam have pets.

Beth and Sam take the dog for a walk.

Mike gives the fish a little bit to eat.

4. How are Beth and Sam alike?

○ They take the dog for a walk.

○ They fill the tank with fish.

○ They fill the cat's dish.

5. How are Beth, Sam, and Mike alike?

○ They all walk the dog.

○ They all have pets.

○ They all pet the cat.

Making Generalizations

Read about ducks. Look at the pictures. Then read each question. Fill in the circle next to the best answer.

Ducks

Ducks live all over the world.
These ducks live where it is cold.
They swim and dive.
They dive to get things to eat,
    such as bugs, clams, and fish.
Ducks that dive have long bills.

These ducks live near a pond.
They swim, but they don't dive.
They eat things such as grass
    and bugs.
Their bills are flat and not
    so long.

Go on

Like all birds, ducks have wings.

Not all birds can fly, but all ducks can fly!

When it gets cold, some ducks fly away.

Some fly for many, many miles.

1. What kind of animal is a duck?

○ a fish

○ a drake

○ a bird

2. Where do all ducks live?

○ many miles away

○ in places that are wet

○ near ponds

3. What is true about ducks?

- ○ All ducks **do** look the same.
- ○ All ducks **don't** look the same.
- ○ All ducks have long bills.

4. Which sentence tells about what ducks eat?

- ○ Ducks don't eat bugs.
- ○ Ducks eat many things.
- ○ Ducks swim, but they don't eat.

5. What do you think helps a duck swim?

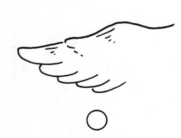

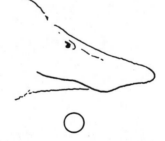

○   ○   ○

STOP

I Name_____

Cause and Effect

Read each part of the story. Then read each
question. Fill in the circle next to the best answer.

Puck

Puck is a good dog.
But once he did a bad thing.
He got Dad's good blue hat.
Puck hid the hat in his bed.
Dad couldn't find his hat!
Dad didn't like that!

1. **Why can't Dad find his hat?**

   ○ **The hat is blue.**
   ○ **Puck is a good dog.**
   ○ **The hat is in Puck's bed.**

2. **How does that make Dad feel?**

   ○ **Dad doesn't like it.**
   ○ **Dad is good.**
   ○ **Dad is glad.**

One other time, Puck was in my room.

Mom called, "Time for your bath, Puck!"

Puck doesn't like baths, so he hid in a box.

"Where is Puck?" asked Mom.

"Puck doesn't like baths," I said.

"Can he skip it this time?"

3. Why does Mom call Puck?

○ to give him a box

○ to give him a bath

○ to get the girl

4. Why does Puck hide in the box?

   ○ Puck doesn't like Mom.
   ○ Puck likes the box.
   ○ Puck doesn't like baths.

5. Why does the girl ask if Puck can skip his bath?

   ○ She knows Puck doesn't like baths.
   ○ She doesn't like Puck.
   ○ She can't find Puck.

J

Name_____

Spelling

Read the sentence with the missing word. Find the right way to spell the word. Fill in the circle next to your answer.

1. I _____ my friend Jane.

    ○ lik
    ○ like
    ○ lak

2. Once Jane _____ to my house to play.

    ○ cam
    ○ caem
    ○ came

Go on

3. _____ had some jacks in a bag.

○ She

○ che

○ Shee

4. We played a _____, but I did not win.

○ gaem

○ gam

○ game

5. Jane and I had a good _____.

○ timm

○ time

○ teim

Name_____

Grammar

Read each question. Fill in the circle next to the best answer.

1. Which one of these is an exclamation?

   ○ I am going to fly my kite today.
   ○ Would you like to come with me?
   ○ Look at that kite fly!

2. Which one of these is an asking sentence?

   ○ Do not let the string go.
   ○ Did your dad make the kite?
   ○ What fun this is!

3. Which one of these is a telling sentence?

   ○ Is today a good day for kites?
   ○ A day with wind is best for kites.
   ○ Here comes some wind!

Go on

Read each sentence. Then fill in the circle next to the word that makes sense in the sentence.

4. Dale said, "_____ can not go on that bike."

   ○ I
   ○ Me
   ○ Them

5. Dad said, "You can go with _____!"

   ○ I
   ○ he
   ○ me

Name_____

Writing Skills

Read each group of words. Fill in the circle next to the complete sentence.

1. ○ We look for shells.
   ○ Mom and I
   ○ for shells

2. ○ a pink shell
   ○ Mom finds a pink shell.
   ○ Mom

3. ○ a clam
   ○ I see a clam.
   ○ a clam in a shell

4. ○ a wave
   ○ comes up and gets
   ○ A wave gets me wet.

5. ○ Mom and I
   ○ Mom smiles at me.
   ○ smiles at me

Animal Adventures
Level 1, Theme 6
Theme Skills Test Record

Student _____ Date _____

Student Record Form

	Possible Score	Criterion Score	Student Score
Part A: Long *o* (CV, CVC*e*) and Long *u* (CVC*e*)	10	8	
Part B: Final Clusters *ft*, *lk*, *nt*	10	8	
Part C: Long *e* (CV, CVC*e*) and Vowel Pairs *ee*, *ea*, *ai*, *ay*	10	8	
Part D: High-Frequency Words	5	4	
Part E: Story Structure	5	4	
Part F: Noting Details	5	4	
Part G: Making Predictions	5	4	
Part H: Spelling	5	4	
Part I: Grammar	5	4	
Part J: Writing Skills	5	4	
TOTAL	65	52	

Total Student Score x 1.54 = _____ %

Long *o* (CV, CVC*e*) and Long *u* (CVC*e*)

Read each sentence. Then fill in the circle next to the word that makes sense in the sentence.

1. Josh gives his dog Shep a _____.

   ○ bond
   ○ bone
   ○ bun

2. Josh's dog is _____!

   ○ honk
   ○ hug
   ○ huge

3. Shep has a wet _____.

   ○ nice
   ○ not
   ○ nose

4. Josh plays with Shep. Shep tugs on a

_____.

○ ripe
○ rope
○ rip

5. Shep sings when Josh plays the _____!

○ flute
○ fine
○ flip

6. Josh thinks Shep is so _____.

○ cut
○ cubs
○ cute

Go on ⇒

7. Shep likes to _____ for walks.

○ go
○ get
○ got

8. He stops to sniff a _____.

○ rise
○ rose
○ rock

9. Josh tells Shep, "_____!"

○ No
○ Note
○ So

10. "Let's go _____," Josh tells Shep.

○ ham
○ hum
○ home

STOP

Final Clusters *ft*, *lk*, *nt*

Read each sentence. Then fill in the circle next to the word that makes sense in the sentence.

1. "Gram _____ this here for you," said Mom.

   ○ less
   ○ left
   ○ let

2. "Do you know what it is?" asked Mom. "It is little and _____," she said.

   ○ soft
   ○ sand
   ○ song

3. "It's as soft as _____," said Mom.

- ○ sing
- ○ sink
- ○ silk

4. "If it's little and soft, it's **not** a _____," said Skip.

- ○ plant
- ○ cat
- ○ pet

5. "You can give it a little bit of _____ to drink," Mom said.

- ○ mill
- ○ mint
- ○ milk

Go on →

6. "It also likes to _____ for mice," said Mom.

- ○ hut
- ○ hunt
- ○ hang

7. "I think I know what it is!" said Skip.

"_____ up the top and let me see it."

- ○ Lift
- ○ Long
- ○ Land

8. "What a good _____ !" Skip said.

- ○ gill
- ○ gift
- ○ gasp

Go on ⟩

9. Skip _____ to write Gram a note.

○ when
○ wind
○ went

10. Then he _____ the note to Gram.

○ sift
○ sent
○ bent

STOP

C

Name_____

Long *e* (CV, CVC*e*); Vowel Pairs *ee*, *ea*, *ai*, *ay*

Read each sentence. Then fill in the circle next to the word that makes sense in the sentence.

1. Mom, Jean, and Pete went to the _____.

   ○ batch
   ○ bee
   ○ beach

2. Mom sat down to _____.

   ○ ray
   ○ read
   ○ ride

3. Jean filled a _____ with sand.

- ○ pail
- ○ peel
- ○ pay

4. Pete walked down to the _____.

- ○ say
- ○ sea
- ○ size

Go on

5. "It _____ so cold!" Pete called.

- ○ fails
- ○ feels
- ○ fills

6. "Don't go out where it's _____," Mom called back.

- ○ drip
- ○ day
- ○ deep

7. "_____ came to swim with you, Pete," said Mom.

○ Wet
○ We
○ Way

8. "It's too cold," said Pete. "I want to _____ out."

○ steep
○ stay
○ sail

9. "_____ I play too?" asked Pete.

○ May

○ Me

○ Meet

10. "I think it's going to _____," said Mom.

"Let's go home."

○ reach

○ raft

○ rain

D

Name_____

High-Frequency Words

Read each sentence. Then fill in the circle next to the word that makes sense in the sentence.

1. Many animals live in the _____.

   ○ forest
   ○ far
   ○ found

2. The sun is down, and it is _____ now.

   ○ table
   ○ evening
   ○ been

3. Some of the animals go _____ to hunt.

   ○ wall
   ○ cow
   ○ out

4. Soon they will not be so _____.

   ○ hungry
   ○ by
   ○ horse

5. In the _____, they'll go back to their dens and nests.

   ○ door
   ○ through
   ○ morning

Name_____

Story Structure

Read the story. Then read each question. Fill in the circle next to the best answer. You can look back at the story for help.

Hen Bakes a Cake

One day Hen baked a cake. Then there was a knock at the door. Rat-a-tat-tat! Rat-a-tat-tat!

"May I come in?" asked Cat.

"Yes, you may," said Hen.

Cat sat down to eat. Rat-a-tat-tat! Rat-a-tat-tat! Pig and Dog came to the door. So did two ducks.

"May we come in, too?" they asked.

"You may if you can fit," cheeped Hen.

Rat-a-tat-tat! Rat-a-tat-tat! Three black birds came to the door.

"May we come in?" asked the birds.

"How will you fit in my house?" asked Hen.

"We'll show you!" said the birds. And they did!

1. Where does the story take place?

- ○ at a small pond
- ○ at a den in the forest
- ○ in a room at Hen's house

2. Who is the main character in the story?

○ Pig

○ Hen

○ Cat

3. Who comes to Hen's house?

○ a cat, a pig, a dog, some ducks, and some birds

○ a cat, a pig, and some black fish

○ some mice, a bat, and some snakes

4. What is the problem in the story?

○ who will make the cake

○ what the black birds will eat

○ how to fit all the animals in

5. How is the problem solved?

○ The birds all go home.

○ The birds find a spot to sit.

○ Hen goes out of the house.

F Name_____

Noting Details

Read the story. Then read each question. Fill in the circle next to the best answer. You can look back at the story for help.

Like a Seal

Jean was looking at the seals. "Those seals can swim!" she said to Dad.

"Yes, they can swim," said Dad. "Seals can dive, too. They can dive deep down."

"I wish I could swim like a seal," said Jean.

"You can, Jean," said Dad. "Let's go to the bay. You can learn to swim there. I'll teach you."

Go on ⟹

Jean and Dad went to the bay. Dad showed Jean how to swim. He lay down and kicked his feet. Then he said, "I'll hold you up, Jean. You do the same thing."

Jean did just what Dad said. Soon Dad did not need to hold her.

"Good for you, Jean!" said Dad. "Soon you will swim just like a seal."

Go on ⇒

1. **What can seals do well?**

   ○ swim and run
   ○ swim and dive
   ○ dive and sail

2. **Where are Jean and Dad at the beginning of the story?**

   ○ in a car
   ○ at a pond
   ○ by the sea

3. **What did Jean wish she could do?**

   ○ swim like a seal
   ○ stay there a long time
   ○ go home and play

Go on

4. Where did Dad take Jean to teach her to swim?

   ○ to a lake
   ○ to the bay
   ○ to the tub

5. What did Jean learn to do first?

   ○ kick her feet
   ○ dive down deep
   ○ clap her hands

G Name_____

Making Predictions

Read each part of the story. Then read each question. Fill in the circle next to the best answer.

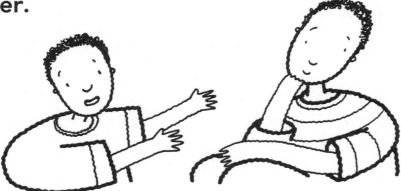

Ted's Wish

Ted wished he could have a pet. One day, he asked his father, "May I get a pet fish, Dad?"

"Yes, you may," said Dad. "But a fish needs to be fed. And it needs a tank to swim in."

"I have a glass tank in my room," said Ted. "And I will feed my fish every day."

1. What do you think Ted's dad will say?

○ "Then you may not get some fish."

○ "Then you may get a fish."

○ "Then you may get some frogs."

So Ted and his father went to the pet shop. They looked at lots of fish.

Ted said, "Look at this blue fish, Dad. And here's one with red dots. But look, Dad. Look at that fish! It has a big fin and black stripes. I like that fish best of all!"

2. Which fish do you think Ted will get?

○ the blue fish
○ the fish with red dots
○ the fish with black stripes

Miss Vine got a bag for the fish. Then she said, "Take this fish home now. It needs to be in a fish tank."

3. Where do you think Ted will go next?

○ home with Dad
○ to the lake
○ to a friend's house

Go on

Ted and Dad drove right home. They filled the fish tank. Then they put Ted's fish into the tank. The fish seemed to like it there.

"Are you hungry, Stripes?" asked Ted.

4. **What do you think Ted will do next?**

○ **feed the fish**

○ **swim in the tank**

○ **take a picture**

"Here you go, Stripes," said Ted. "I will feed you every day. But I also think you need some friends."

5. **What do you think Ted will ask Dad for next?**

○ **a small tank**

○ **more fish**

○ **a frog**

Name_____

Spelling

Read the sentence with the missing word. Find the right way to spell the word. Fill in the circle next to your answer.

1. Let's _____ to the pond!

    ○ go
    ○ goe
    ○ og

2. A pond is _____ to many animals.

    ○ hom
    ○ hoem
    ○ home

Go on

3. You can _____ fish in a pond.

- ○ es
- ○ see
- ○ se

4. You _____ find a frog.

- ○ may
- ○ mai
- ○ miy

5. All these animals need to _____.

- ○ ete
- ○ et
- ○ eat

Grammar

Read each question. Then fill in the circle next to the best answer.

1. Which word names a person?

   ○ horse
   ○ dog
   ○ mother

2. Which word names a place?

   ○ sled
   ○ home
   ○ desk

3. Which word names an animal?

   ○ pond
   ○ pig
   ○ stone

4. Which word names **one** thing?

- ○ rat
- ○ cows
- ○ bugs

5. Which word names **more than one** thing?

- ○ mop
- ○ leaf
- ○ eggs

Name_____

Writing Skills

Read the story. Then read each question.
Fill in the circle next to the best answer.

Fun Pets

It's fun to have a cat for a pet. Cats like to nap in spots where there is sun. Cats like to play with string. Cats also like people to pet them.

It's fun to have a dog for a pet. Dogs chase sticks. They like to go for walks with people. Dogs like people to pet them, too.

1. **What animals are in the story Fun Pets?**

   ○ **Fish and mice are in Fun Pets.**
   ○ **Cats and dogs are in Fun Pets.**
   ○ **Birds and cows are in Fun Pets.**

2. **What is one thing cats like to do?**

   ○ **Cats like to chase sticks.**
   ○ **Cats with spots like dogs.**
   ○ **Cats like to nap in the sun.**

3. What is one thing dogs like to do?

- ○ Dogs like to see spots.
- ○ Dogs like to go for walks.
- ○ Dogs like to pet people.

4. What do people do with dogs and cats?

- ○ People spot dogs and cats.
- ○ People chase dogs and cats.
- ○ People pet dogs and cats.

5. What does the author think about dogs and cats?

- ○ Dogs are good pets but cats are not.
- ○ Dogs are good pets, and so are cats.
- ○ The best pet is a cute dog.

We Can Work It Out
Level 1, Theme 7
Theme Skills Test Record

Student _____ Date _____

Student Record Form

	Possible Score	Criterion Score	Student Score
Part A: Vowel Pairs *oa* and *ow*	10	8	
Part B: The /o͝o/ Sound for *oo*	10	8	
Part C: Compound Words	10	8	
Part D: Vowel Pairs *oo, ew, ue, ou* (/o͞o/)	10	8	
Part E: High-Frequency Words	5	4	
Part F: Problem Solving	5	4	
Part G: Sequence of Events	5	4	
Part H: Fantasy and Realism	5	4	
Part I: Spelling	5	4	
Part J: Grammar	5	4	
Part K: Writing Skills	5	4	
TOTAL	75	60	

Total Student Score x 1.33 = _____ %

Vowel Pairs *oa* and *ow*

Read each sentence. Then fill in the circle next to the word that makes sense in the sentence.

1. "It's a good day to go out in our
   _____," said Joan.

   ○ bow
   ○ boat
   ○ bait

2. "I can feel that wind _____!" said Mom.

   ○ blow
   ○ bowl
   ○ brown

3. "I'm glad we have our _____ on," said Joan.

   ○ cats
   ○ cots
   ○ coats

4. "You rest, Joan," said Mom. "I'll _____."

- ○ ray
- ○ row
- ○ rope

5. "I like a _____ ride," said Joan.

- ○ see
- ○ slap
- ○ slow

6. "We can just _____," said Mom.

- ○ flee
- ○ float
- ○ flat

Go on ⟹

7. "Don't lean over too far," said Mom. "You'll fall in and get _____ wet."

- ○ soaking
- ○ seeking
- ○ snacking

8. "I see Dad on the _____," said Mom.

- ○ read
- ○ road
- ○ rude

9. "The sun is _____, so we must go," said Mom.

○ low
○ lap
○ load

10. "Make a knot," said Mom. "Do not make a _____."

○ bee
○ bank
○ bow

The /o͝o/ Sound for *oo*

Read each sentence. Then fill in the circle next to the word that makes sense in the sentence.

1. Jeff went down to the _____.

   ○ brook

   ○ brake

   ○ broke

2. He _____ his dog King with him.

   ○ take

   ○ tick

   ○ took

3. Jeff had a _____ to read.

    ○ bake

    ○ book

    ○ brick

4. "It's a _____ day to read," he said to King.

    ○ game

    ○ got

    ○ good

5. All King said was, "_____."

    ○ woke

    ○ woof

    ○ who

Go on ➡

6. Jeff sat down to _____ at his book.

- ◯ lock
- ◯ lake
- ◯ look

7. King sat by Jeff's right _____.

- ◯ foot
- ◯ fit
- ◯ flute

8. "Fetch this stick of _____, King," said Jeff.

- ○ cook
- ○ wood
- ○ woke

9. King _____ up and went for the stick.

- ○ stood
- ○ stay
- ○ stone

10. Then he _____ water all over Jeff.

○ shake

○ hook

○ shook

Compound Words

Read each sentence. Then fill in the circle next to
the word that makes sense in the sentence.

1. Meg likes _____ best of all.

   ○ splash
   ○ anyway
   ○ springtime

2. Meg likes to go _____ then.

   ○ outdoors
   ○ doghouse
   ○ beside

3. She wakes up at _____.

- ○ sunrise
- ○ sidewalk
- ○ someday

4. Her _____ fills with sunlight.

- ○ bathtub
- ○ bedroom
- ○ classroom

5. Meg eats _____ so she won't
be hungry.

- ○ pancakes
- ○ pink
- ○ doorway

6. Then she fills her _____ with books.

- ○ backpack
- ○ beanbag
- ○ packed

Go on →

7. Then Meg goes _____ to read.

- ○ ouch
- ○ outside
- ○ other

8. The sun comes up over the _____.

- ○ tugboats
- ○ teacups
- ○ treetops

Go on →

9. _____ Meg stays out all morning.

- ○ **Soon**
- ○ **Someone**
- ○ **Sometimes**

10. She reads books and writes in her _____.

- ○ **never**
- ○ **notebook**
- ○ **nutshell**

Name_____

Vowel Pairs *oo, ew, ue, ou* (/o͞o/)

Read each sentence. Then fill in the circle next to the word that makes sense in the sentence.

1. Last week, our class went to the _____.

    ○ few
    ○ zoom
    ○ zoo

Go on

2. Miss Blane _____ we would learn a lot at the zoo.

   ○ knot
   ○ knew
   ○ knee

3. A mother or a father was with each _____.

   ○ group
   ○ good
   ○ glue

4. We each had a _____ notebook.

   ○ noon
   ○ blue
   ○ scoot

5. Sue asked her dad, "Is it _____ that bears eat fish?"

- ○ true
- ○ too
- ○ troop

6. Her dad said, "Look there! It tells what _____ they eat."

- ○ fade
- ○ tools
- ○ foods

7. Next we went to see seals in a big

_____.

- ○ pole
- ○ pool
- ○ plop

8. Sue said, "Look! They like

fish _____!"

- ○ tree
- ○ trot
- ○ too

9. We all _____ pictures of the animals.

- ○ soup
- ○ drew
- ○ drove

Bears and seals eat fish.

10. We also wrote _____ things
we learned.

- ○ new
- ○ now
- ○ no

Name_____

High-Frequency Words

Read each sentence. Then fill in the circle next to the word that makes sense in the sentence.

1. "Where are my _____?" asked Drew.

   ○ most
   ○ start
   ○ shoes

2. "_____ of them are gone!" he shouted.

   ○ Build
   ○ Both
   ○ Hard

Go on

3. "Did you look _____ the bed?" asked Mom.

○ under
○ very
○ turn

4. "Yes, but I'll look _____," said Drew.

○ afraid
○ any
○ again

5. "That was a good _____!" said Drew.

○ idea
○ water
○ bear

Name_____

Problem Solving

Read the story and look at the pictures. Then read each question. Fill in the circle next to the best answer. You can look back at the story for help.

What Can We Do?

June and Jane look the same. Many times, they think the same, too. But this is not one of those days.

Today, June wants to run at the track. Jane wants to ride bikes. The girls do not have time to do both things!

Go on ⇒

"Let's run today," June tells Jane. "We can ride our bikes on Sunday."

"No," calls Jane. "Let's ride today and run some other time."

"No!" yells Jane. "I want to run!"

"I know what we can do," Jane tells June. "I can ride, and you can run beside me."

June thinks that is a very good idea.

1. What is the problem at the beginning of the story?

○ June and Jane look the same.
○ June and Jane both have bikes.
○ June and Jane do not want to do the same thing.

2. At first, what does June say they should do?

○ ask their mother to tell them what to do
○ run today and ride bikes on Sunday
○ ride bikes on the track

3. At first, what does Jane say they should do?

○ ride bikes today and run some other day

○ run and ride bikes today

○ not do anything today

4. How do the girls fix the problem?

○ One runs and the other rides.

○ Both girls run.

○ Both girls ride their bikes.

5. How do you think the girls feel at the end?

○ June is sad.

○ Both girls feel good.

○ They don't like each other anymore.

Sequence of Events

Read the story and look at the pictures. Then read each question. Fill in the circle next to the best answer. You can look back at the story for help.

Where Is Glen?

Mother Hen had six little ones. When it was time to eat, she called them. "One, two, three, four, five," she said. "Someone is not here. I see Ben, Ken, Jen, Pen, and Len. But where is little Glen?"

Go on ⟩

First, they all called Glen. Then they looked under trees and plants. But they did not find Glen.

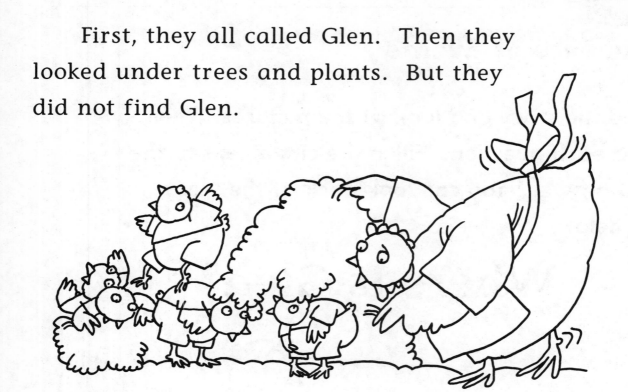

At last, Mother Hen looked down. What did she see? Little tracks!

"I will follow these tracks," she said. "They will lead me to Glen."

Go on ▷

Mother hen followed the tracks. Ben, Ken,
Jen, Pen, and Len followed.   And there was
Glen, eating a snack!

1. **Which picture shows what happens at the
beginning of the story?**

○   ○   ○

Go on ⇨

2. What does the family do first to find Glen?

○ They call him.
○ They look under trees and plants.
○ They look in the house.

3. What do they do next?

○ They give little Glen big hugs.
○ They look under trees and plants.
○ They eat a snack.

4. What does Mother Hen do when she finds the tracks?

○ She calls Ben, Ken, Jen, Pen, and Len.
○ She calls, "One, two, three, four, five."
○ She follows the tracks.

5. What happens at the end of the story?

○ They find Glen eating a snack.
○ They can't find Glen.
○ They all lead Mother Hen home.

Fantasy and Realism

Read the story. Then read each question. Fill in the circle next to the best answer. You can look back at the story for help.

Moon Trip

"Look at the moon!" Cat said to Rat. "What do you think it's made of, Rat?"

"I would say cheese," said Cat's friend, Rat. "Or maybe it's made of cat food. Who knows?"

"It doesn't look like cat food to me," said Cat. "The best cat food is fish. That moon is not the right color for fish."

"Well, why don't we go find out?" asked Rat.

"How will we get there?" asked Cat.

"Follow me, my friend," said Rat.

"What a ride!" yelled Cat, so Rat could hear.

"Hold on now!" Rat called back.

Soon the spaceship was landing on the moon. Once it had landed, Cat and Rat got out. Each picked up a piece of moon rock.

"What do you think, Rat?" asked Cat.

"It doesn't look like cheese," said Rat.

"And it doesn't smell like fish," said Cat.

"I think that if we want to eat, we must go home," said Rat.

And that's just what they did.

Go on

1. What does the cat do that **could** be real?

   ○ The cat speaks.
   ○ The cat goes to the moon.
   ○ The cat likes to eat cat food.

2. What does the rat do that **could** be real?

   ○ The rat likes the smell of cheese.
   ○ The rat speaks to a cat.
   ○ The rat drives a spaceship.

3. What does the cat do that **could not** be real?

   ○ The cat sees a rat.
   ○ The cat likes to eat fish.
   ○ The cat visits the moon.

Go on ⟹

4. What does the rat do that **could not** be real?

   ○ The rat likes the smell of cheese.
   ○ The rat tells the cat, "Let's go home."
   ○ The rat eats.

5. Which **could** be real?

   ○ A rat calls, "Hold on now!"
   ○ A cat yells, "What a ride!"
   ○ A spaceship goes to the moon.

Spelling

Read the sentence with the missing word. Find the right way to spell the word. Fill in the circle next to your answer.

1. **Rose wanted to learn to _____.**

   ○ kook
   ○ cook
   ○ kuk

2. **Her dad said, "I will _____ you how."**

   ○ show
   ○ shoa
   ○ sho

3. "What _____ do you want to make?"
he asked.

- ◯ fod
- ◯ foud
- ◯ food

4. "I don't know," said Rose. "Something we
can eat _____!"

- ◯ soon
- ◯ soun
- ◯ sonn

5. "I'll _____ you how to make soup,"
said Dad.

- ◯ shou
- ◯ sho
- ◯ show

J

Name_____

Grammar

Read each question. Fill in the circle next to the best answer.

1. Which word is a **special naming word** for a person?

   ○ sun
   ○ Sue
   ○ girl

2. Which word is a **special naming word** for a pet?

   ○ dog
   ○ cat
   ○ Spot

3. Which word is a **special naming word** for a place?

   ○ tree
   ○ Blue Lake
   ○ pond

Go on

Read each sentence. Fill in the circle next to the word that can take the place of the underlined naming word.

4. <u>Jim</u> likes to skate on the lake.

   ○ He
   ○ It
   ○ They

5. Did <u>the lake</u> freeze over yet?

   ○ she
   ○ it
   ○ they

K Name_____

Writing Skills

Read each sentence. Then choose a naming word that tells more to replace the underlined word. Fill in the circle next to the best answer.

1. I want to get a <u>pet</u>.

   ○ thing

   ○ father

   ○ dog

2. I need <u>someone</u> to take me to the pet shop.

   ○ he

   ○ Dad

   ○ people

3. Dad and I ride on a thing.

    ○ bus

    ○ bird

    ○ cat

4. Dad tells me we can find a dog in this place.

    ○ beach

    ○ pet shop

    ○ picnic

5. We see many dogs and things there.

    ○ children

    ○ they

    ○ cats

Our Earth
Level 1, Theme 8
Theme Skills Test Record

Student _____ Date _____

Student Record Form

	Possible Score	Criterion Score	Student Score
Part A: Base Words and Endings *-s*, *-ed*, *-ing*	10	8	
Part B: Vowel Pairs *ou*, *ow*	10	8	
Part C: Base Words and Endings *-ed*, *-ing*	10	8	
Part D: High-Frequency Words	5	4	
Part E: Categorize and Classify	5	4	
Part F: Topic, Main Idea, Details/Summarizing	5	4	
Part G: Drawing Conclusions	5	4	
Part H: Spelling	5	4	
Part I: Grammar	5	4	
Part J: Writing Skills	5	4	
TOTAL	65	52	

Total Student Score x 1.54 = _____ %

Base Words and Endings *-s*, *-ed*, *-ing*

Read each sentence. Then fill in the circle next to the word that makes sense in the sentence.

1. In the evening, the sun _____.

   ○ sets

   ○ setting

   ○ sees

2. The moon _____, and stars come out.

   ○ singing

   ○ shines

   ○ shine

Go on

3. My family and I like _____ out then.

    ○ going
    ○ goes
    ○ growing

4. One evening we _____ up at a full moon.

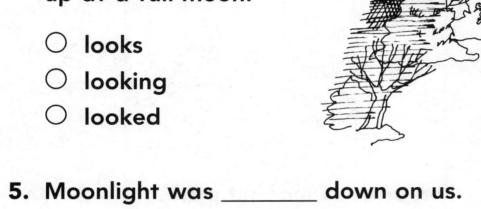

    ○ looks
    ○ looking
    ○ looked

5. Moonlight was _____ down on us.

    ○ beaming
    ○ beamed
    ○ beam

6. Dad _____ to go for a walk in the woods.

    ○ wanting
    ○ wanted
    ○ want

7. We _____ him down a moonlit path.

   ○ following

   ○ follows

   ○ followed

8. "Do you hear that?" Dad _____.

   ○ asked

   ○ asking

   ○ ask

9. Some kind of bird was _____.

   ○ hoots

   ○ hooting

   ○ hooted

10. "Do you think it is _____ to us?" asked Dad.

   ○ called

   ○ calls

   ○ calling

Vowel Pairs *ou*, *ow* (/ou/)

Read each sentence. Then fill in the circle next to the word that makes sense in the sentence.

1. My pet is a black and white _____ dog.

   ○ how
   ○ hound
   ○ hand

2. We are so glad we _____ her.

   ○ found
   ○ friend
   ○ flower

3. Now she lives in our _____.

○ hose
○ house
○ hails

4. Once she got up onto the _____.

○ couch
○ catch
○ cast

Go on ⇨

5. "Get _____ right now!"
   Dad yelled.

   ○ drain
   ○ drum
   ○ down

6. That dog jumped down fast
   when Dad _____!

   ○ shouted
   ○ shut
   ○ shopped

7. Our dog does another thing
   Dad does not like. She digs
   holes in the _____.

   ○ grand
   ○ ground
   ○ grin

Go on

8. When we go out and leave her, she _____.

- ○ howls
- ○ how
- ○ hails

9. We think she is very _____.

- ○ land
- ○ lost
- ○ loud

10. I like my dog, but I don't like such a loud

_____.

- ○ stand
- ○ sound
- ○ spend

C   Name_____

Base Words and Endings *-ed*, *-ing*

Read each sentence. Look at the underlined
word. Find the base word for that word. Fill in
the circle next to your answer.

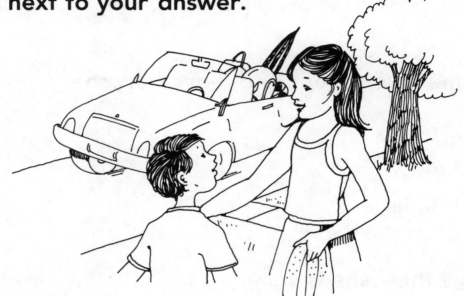

1. "Do you want to go <u>swimming</u>?" asked Tish.

    ○ win
    ○ swim
    ○ swing

2. The sun was <u>shining</u>, so I said, "Yes."

    ○ shine
    ○ ship
    ○ shin

3. But <u>driving</u> to the beach took a long time.

- ○ dive
- ○ drove
- ○ drive

4. By the time we got there, the rain was <u>coming</u> down.

- ○ climb
- ○ come
- ○ cone

5. Tish said, "Well, it's no fun just <u>sitting</u> in the car."

- ○ sit
- ○ site
- ○ it

6. "I have an idea," she <u>added</u>.

- ○ did
- ○ an
- ○ add

Go on

7. "I think you want to go <u>shopping</u>!" I said.

   ○ ping
   ○ shop
   ○ shape

8. "You will like the shop I'm <u>thinking</u> of," she said.

   ○ thin
   ○ king
   ○ think

9. She <u>smiled</u> and said, "How about some ice cream?"

   ○ smile
   ○ mile
   ○ smell

10. We both <u>hopped</u> out of the car and ran.

   ○ hope
   ○ hop
   ○ hot

D Name_____

High-Frequency Words

Read each sentence. Then fill in the circle next to the word that makes sense in the sentence.

1. Lou likes to _____ pictures.

○ arms

○ saw

○ draw

2. In class, he does his _____ well.

○ were

○ work

○ warm

---

3. He _____ does his math.

   ○ always
   ○ about
   ○ eight

4. Our _____ says he spells like a champ.

   ○ tiny
   ○ part
   ○ teacher

5. But drawing is what makes Lou _____!

   ○ body
   ○ because
   ○ happy

Name_____

Categorize and Classify

Read the story. Then read each question. Fill in the circle next to the best answer. You can look back at the story for help.

When it rains, you may need to play indoors. What can you do indoors? You can play a game with a friend. You can build something with blocks. You can learn how to bake a cake.

Go on

When the sun shines, it's fun to go out. You can do lots of things outdoors. You can play a game with friends. You can swing. You can look for flowers to pick. You can learn how to skate.

1. What things can you do indoors?

○ skate, bake a cake, pick flowers

○ bake a cake, play a game, build with blocks

○ swing, play a game, skate

2. What things can you do outdoors?

○ build with blocks, play a game, bake a cake

○ bake a cake, skate, swing

○ swing, skate, pick flowers

Go on

3. What can you do indoors and outdoors?

- ○ play games
- ○ pick flowers
- ○ bake a cake

4. What is a good name for this picture?

- ○ Places
- ○ People
- ○ Games

5. What is a good title for this selection?

- ○ Games Children Like
- ○ Fun Indoors and Outdoors
- ○ Learning to Skate

Name_____

Topic, Main Idea, Details/Summarizing

Read the story. Then read each question. Fill in the circle next to the best answer. You can look back at the story for help.

From Tadpole to Frog

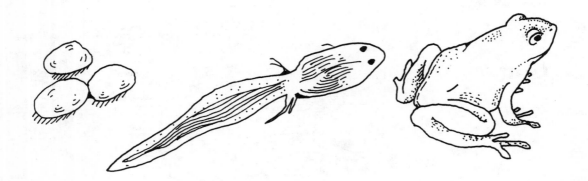

    A mother frog lays her eggs in water. The eggs hatch into tadpoles. At first, tadpoles look like fish. They have gills and tails, just as fish do. They do not have legs or lungs yet. As tadpoles grow up, they get legs and lungs. They also lose their gills and tails. Then they can live on land, just like big frogs. It's fun to see a tadpole grow up!

Go on ⟹

1. What is the topic of this selection?

○ animals
○ fish
○ tadpoles

2. What is the main idea of the selection?

○ Fish can live in water because they have gills.
○ A tadpole grows up to become a frog.
○ Frogs can live on land.

3. Which of these is a detail in the selection?

○ When tadpoles first hatch, they look like fish.
○ Fish cannot live on land.
○ Frogs can be green or spotted brown in color.

4. Which of these is a detail in the selection?

○ Most frogs live near ponds and streams.

○ Fish need gills so that they can breathe.

○ As tadpoles grow up, they get legs and lungs.

5. Which is the best summary of the selection?

○ Tadpoles swim like fish, but they aren't fish.

○ Frog eggs hatch into tadpoles that change and grow up to be frogs.

○ Some animals live on land, while others live in water.

STOP

Name_____

Drawing Conclusions

Read each part of the story. Then read each question. Fill in the circle next to the best answer.

Sue Gets Her Wish

"Mom, may I go out to play?" asked Sue.

"Not now," said Mom. "I don't want you to get wet. But the sun may be out in the morning. If it is, we'll go on a little trip."

1. Why couldn't Sue go out to play?

   ○ Her friends were not home.

   ○ It was time for bed.

   ○ It was raining.

 Go on

When Sue woke up, she looked out.
"Good, good, GOOD!" she said.

2. What did Sue see when she looked out?

- ○ the sun shining
- ○ more rain
- ○ the moon shining

Sue jumped out of bed and got dressed.
She went to find her mother. Sue's mom was
packing a bag.

3. How do you think Sue felt when she saw Mom packing?

- ○ mad
- ○ happy
- ○ sad

"Who wants to go on a trip?"
asked Mom.

"I do!" said Sue. She ran to Mom
and hugged her.

4. Why did Sue hug her mother?

○ Mom was taking her on a trip.

○ Mom was making her a cake.

○ Mom was going to work.

5. Where do you think Sue and Mom went?

○ to a pet shop

○ to the playground

○ to the beach

Name_____

Spelling

Read the sentence with the missing word. Find the right way to spell the word. Fill in the circle next to your answer.

1. Mom calls, "The plane has _____!"

    ○ landed
    ○ landd
    ○ ladnd

2. Gramps does not step _____ of the jet.

    ○ ow
    ○ out
    ○ owt

Go on ⇒

3. We say, "Maybe he _____ the plane!"

- ◯ misst
- ◯ mised
- ◯ missed

4. Then Mom tells us, "See that man with the toy _____?"

- ◯ fogg
- ◯ fros
- ◯ frogs

5. "Oh, good! We can see Gramps _____," we say.

- ◯ nou
- ◯ kno
- ◯ now

Name_____

Grammar

Read each question. Then fill in the circle next to the best answer.

1. What is the action word in this sentence?
    The children eat their lunch.

    ○ eat
    ○ lunch
    ○ children

2. What is the action word in this sentence?
    Nan walked to the bus stop every day
    last week.

    ○ Nan
    ○ week
    ○ walked

3. What is the action word in this sentence?
Tim stayed home sick last week.

- ○ home
- ○ stayed
- ○ Tim

4. Which word tells about an action that is happening now?

- ○ learned
- ○ speak
- ○ played

5. Which word tells about an action that already happened?

- ○ paint
- ○ paints
- ○ painted

Writing Skills

Read each sentence. Then choose the clearest action word to complete each sentence.
Fill in the circle next to the best answer.

1. Tom doesn't want to be late, so he _____ to the bus stop.

   ○ gets
   ○ goes
   ○ races

2. When the bus pulls up, Tom _____ up the steps.

   ○ goes
   ○ climbs
   ○ gets

Go on

3. He _____ himself down in a back seat.

    ○ lets

    ○ plops

    ○ sits

4. "Oh, no!" _____ Tom. "I forgot my homework!"

    ○ shouts

    ○ goes

    ○ speaks

5. Tom _____ back into his seat and groans.

    ○ sits

    ○ goes

    ○ falls

Special Friends
Level 1, Theme 9
Theme Skills Test Record

Student _____   Date _____

Student Record Form

	Possible Score	Criterion Score	Student Score
Part A: Sounds for *y*	10	8	
Part B: Base Words and Endings *-es, -ies*	10	8	
Part C: Vowel Pairs: *oi, oy, aw, au*	10	8	
Part D: High-Frequency Words	5	4	
Part E: Noting Details	5	4	
Part F: Story Structure	5	4	
Part G: Compare and Contrast	5	4	
Part H: Spelling	5	4	
Part I: Grammar	5	4	
Part J: Writing Skills	5	4	
TOTAL	65	52	

Total Student Score x 1.54 = _____ %

Name_____

Sounds for *y*

Read each sentence. Then fill in the circle next to the word that makes sense in the sentence.

1. Here is a picture of our new _____.

   ○ by
   ○ baby
   ○ bay

2. Now there are four people in my _____.

   ○ fishy
   ○ fly
   ○ family

3. She is little, but she is not _____.

   ○ shine
   ○ shy
   ○ she

4. She makes Mom very _____.

- ○ hay
- ○ hilly
- ○ happy

5. But she does know how to _____!

- ○ cry
- ○ carry
- ○ fly

6. I do not know _____ she is crying.

- ○ windy
- ○ why
- ○ we

7. I think she may be _____.

- ○ Billy
- ○ hazy
- ○ hungry

Go on

8. I _____ to make her stop.

- ○ funny
- ○ dry
- ○ try

9. I make _____ faces.

- ○ silly
- ○ sandy
- ○ pretty

10. She is a _____ baby, don't you think?

- ○ many
- ○ lucky
- ○ lick

Name

Base Words and Endings *-es*, *-ies*

Read each sentence. Then fill in the circle next to the word that makes sense in the sentence.

1. Some _____ have more than one pet.

   ○ fishes
   ○ families
   ○ family

2. We got our two dogs when they were _____.

   ○ puppies
   ○ pages
   ○ puppy

3. We got two _____ for their food.

   ○ dish
   ○ dishes
   ○ dresses

4. We made two _____ for their beds.

- ○ box
- ○ bosses
- ○ boxes

5. We got two _____ for walking the dogs.

- ○ reaches
- ○ leashes
- ○ leash

6. Mom _____ the dogs new tricks.

- ○ teaches
- ○ bunches
- ○ teach

7. Spot _____ a ball.

- ○ peaches
- ○ catch
- ○ catches

Go on ⟹

8. Patches _____ after a stick.

- ◯ chases
- ◯ chase
- ◯ matches

9. The dogs make _____ while we are away.

- ◯ misses
- ◯ mess
- ◯ messes

10. But when we come home, they jump up and give us _____.

- ◯ lunches
- ◯ kisses
- ◯ kiss

C Name_____

Vowel Pairs: *oi*, *oy*, *aw*, *au*

Read each sentence. Then fill in the circle next to the word that makes sense in the sentence.

1. My friend is a little _____ named Paul.

   ○ base
   ○ boy
   ○ bone

2. One day he came to help us pull up weeds in the _____.

   ○ lake
   ○ law
   ○ lawn

Go on

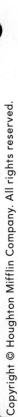

3. Paul looked around and _____ something
he could do.

- ○ sauce
- ○ saw
- ○ save

4. He pulled a few green things out of
the _____.

- ○ soil
- ○ sail
- ○ seal

5. All at once, we could hear Mom's _____.

- ○ vote
- ○ vase
- ○ voice

6. "Stop, Paul!" she said. "You will _____ the garden!"

    ○ spill

    ○ spoil

    ○ spring

7. Then Mom _____ to some writing.

    ○ pointed

    ○ painted

    ○ pot

8. "It's not your _____, Paul," she said.

    ○ fall

    ○ faint

    ○ fault

9. "I will _____ pictures on the tags," she added.

- ○ draw
- ○ dream
- ○ drove

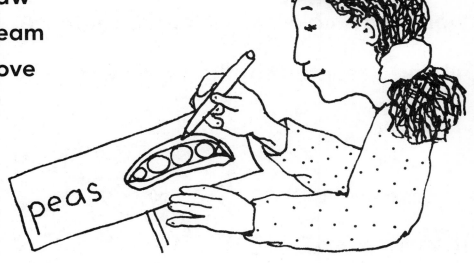

10. Then Mom gave Paul a _____ to play with.

- ○ too
- ○ toy
- ○ tot

STOP

Name_____

High-Frequency Words

Read each sentence. Then fill in the circle next to the word that makes sense in the sentence.

1. Jill and I wanted to plant a flower _____.

    ○ around
    ○ ocean
    ○ garden

2. Dad took us to the shop to _____ seeds.

    ○ before
    ○ buy
    ○ baby

3. There were so many _____ flowers we could choose.

    ○ open
    ○ only
    ○ pretty

4. Jill and I worked _____ to plant the seeds.

- ○ school
- ○ though
- ○ together

5. It was the most fun I have _____ had.

- ○ off
- ○ after
- ○ ever

Noting Details

Read the story. Then read each question. Fill in
the circle next to the best answer. You can look
back at the story for help.

After School

My name is Joy. I am six.
I live in a big tan building.
Sally is my best friend. She
is seven. Sally comes over
every day after school.

Sally and I like to sing
and dance and paint. We
like painting the best. Sally
likes to paint big shapes.

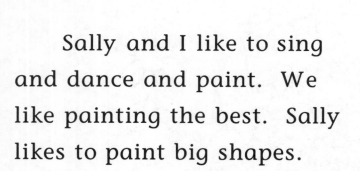

Go on ⟹

When it rains, we like to tell tales. I know a long tale about a cat and a boy. Sally likes to hear the tale three times in a row!

Sally's aunt picks her up at night. They go home to her house. I can't wait to paint with Sally again!

1. Who is six years old?

- ○ **Mom**
- ○ **Joy**
- ○ **Sally**

2. Where do the girls go every day after school?

- ○ to Sally's house
- ○ to school
- ○ to where Joy lives

3. What do the girls like to do best of all?

- ○ sing
- ○ paint
- ○ dance

4. When do the girls tell tales?

- ○ when it rains
- ○ when it is sunny
- ○ when they are sad

5. How many times does Joy tell her tale?

- ○ two times
- ○ one time
- ○ three times

STOP

F

Name_____

Story Structure

Read the story and look at the pictures. Then read each question. Fill in the circle next to the best answer. You can look back at the story for help.

On the Pond

Fred Frog lived in a pond. He liked being in the water. The pond was a good place to swim and look around.

One day, Bud Bird came to see his friend Fred. Bud and Fred liked to talk.

"Hi Fred," said Bud Bird. "It is a good day."

"Yes, it is," said Fred Frog.

Go on →

"What a day. The sun is shining," said Fred Frog.

"It is hot now. How is the pond?" asked Bud Bird.

"It feels good," said Fred Frog.

"I wish I could go in the pond," said Bud Bird. "But I can't swim."

"Wait," said Fred Frog, "I know what to do."

Go on

Fred Frog got a lily pad and pushed it to the side. Bud Bird got on. The lily pad was like a boat. Bud Bird had fun.

"It is not so hot out here on the water," said Bud Bird. "Thank you, Fred Frog. This is so much fun!"

1. **Where does the story take place?**

    ○ at a beach
    ○ at a lake
    ○ at a pond

2. Who are the main characters?

○ Bud Bird
○ Bud Bird and Fred Frog
○ Fred Frog

3. What do Fred and Bud like to do together?

○ talk
○ eat
○ swim

4. What is Bud's problem?

○ He can't talk to his friend Fred.
○ He can't go in the water to cool off.
○ He has no friends.

5. How does Fred help Bud solve his problem?

○ He tells Bud to jump in the water anyway.
○ He teaches Bud to swim.
○ He gets a lily pad for Bud to float on.

G

Name

Compare and Contrast

Read the story. Then read each question. Fill in the circle next to the best answer. You can look back at the story for help.

Good Friends

Matt, Deb, and Roy are good friends. They are alike in many ways. They all live on the same street. They all like to eat hot dogs. Matt, Deb, and Roy like to read books and play games.

Go on

But Matt, Deb, and Roy are not alike in **every** way. Roy and Deb are ten. Matt is six.

Roy likes to fly kites.

Deb and Matt like
to play ball.

Matt likes to ride his
bike. Roy and Deb like
to skate. Matt can't skate.

1. How are Roy, Deb, and Matt alike?

○ **They are all boys.**
○ **They are all the same age.**
○ **They live on the same street.**

2. What is one thing Roy, Deb, and Matt all like to do?

○ They all like to eat hot dogs.
○ They all like to skate.
○ They all like to fly kites.

3. How is Roy different from Deb and Matt?

○ Roy doesn't eat hot dogs.
○ Roy can't read.
○ Roy flies kites.

4. How is Matt different from Roy and Deb?

○ Matt can't skate.
○ Matt likes to play games.
○ Matt likes to read books.

5. How are Deb and Roy alike?

○ They are both ten.
○ They are both girls.
○ They are both six.

Spelling

Read the sentence with the missing word. Find the right way to spell the word. Fill in the circle next to your answer.

1. Our new baby is a _____.

    ○ boi

    ○ boiy

    ○ boy

2. Our baby will sometimes _____.

    ○ crie

    ○ cry

    ○ cri

3. I don't know _____ he does that.

   ○ whi
   ○ why
   ○ y

4. I give him lots of _____.

   ○ kisses
   ○ kises
   ○ kissis

5. Maybe he wants my _____.

   ○ toyy
   ○ toi
   ○ toy

I Name_____

Grammar

Read each sentence. Then fill in the circle next to the word that makes sense in the sentence.

1. There _____ three kites in the sky now.

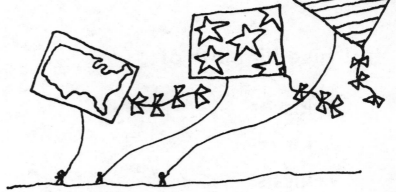

   ○ are
   ○ is
   ○ was

2. Last week, there _____ only two kites here.

   ○ is
   ○ were
   ○ was

3. Right now, there _____ a new kite with stripes.

   ○ were
   ○ is
   ○ was

Go on ⇨

Read each question. Fill in the circle next to the best answer.

4. Which word tells the number of kites you see?

○ round
○ blue
○ three

5. Which word tells the size of the kites?

○ white
○ five
○ big

Writing Skills

Look at the picture and read the sentence. Then choose an action part or a naming part to complete the sentence. Fill in the circle next to the best answer.

1. _____ play in the sand.

   ○ Walk
   ○ The boys
   ○ Run

2. The girl _____ to the water.

   ○ runs
   ○ father
   ○ ball

3. _____ goes with her.

   ○ Play
   ○ Follow
   ○ Her father

Read each question. Fill in the circle next to the best answer.

4. Which of these is a **complete sentence?**

   ○ the little girl
   ○ splashes her father
   ○ She splashes her father.

5. Which of these is a **complete sentence?**

   ○ her father
   ○ He feels cold.
   ○ feels very cold

We Can Do It!
Level 1, Theme 10
Theme Skills Test Record

Student _____ Date _____

Student Record Form

	Possible Score	Criterion Score	Student Score
Part A: r-Controlled Vowels: *or*, *ore*	10	8	
Part B: r-Controlled Vowels: *er*, *ir*, *ur*	10	8	
Part C: r-Controlled Vowels: *ar*	10	8	
Part D: Base Words and Endings *-er*, *-est*	10	8	
Part E: High-Frequency Words	5	4	
Part F: Making Predictions	5	4	
Part G: Sequence of Events	5	4	
Part H: Cause and Effect	5	4	
Part I: Spelling	5	4	
Part J: Grammar	5	4	
Part K: Writing Skills	5	4	
TOTAL	75	60	

Total Student Score x 1.33 = %

r-Controlled Vowels: *or*, *ore*

1. I am something you eat with. I am a
_____.

- ◯ fork
- ◯ fort
- ◯ fake

2. I am the opposite of **tall**. I am _____.

- ◯ shot
- ◯ sheet
- ◯ short

3. I am a building where you buy things. I am a
_____.

- ◯ steam
- ◯ store
- ◯ street

4. I am the place where the ocean meets the land. I am the _____.

- ○ shore
- ○ shoe
- ○ show

5. I have lots of wind and rain. I am a _____.

- ○ stream
- ○ stem
- ○ storm

6. I tell you who won the game. I am the _____.

- ○ stop
- ○ score
- ○ scrap

7. I am something to eat. I am _____.

- ○ color
- ○ chin
- ○ corn

Go on

8. I am part of a house. I am outside. I am a

_____.

- ○ porch
- ○ patch
- ○ pouch

9. I grow on the stem of a rose. I am a

_____.

- ○ thin
- ○ thorn
- ○ those

10. I go beep, beep, BEEP! I am a _____.

- ○ hose
- ○ hear
- ○ horn

B   Name_____

r-Controlled Vowels: *er*, *ir*, *ur*

Read each sentence. Then fill in the circle next to the word that makes sense in the sentence.

1. _____ like to come to Mort's garden.

   ○ Bikes
   ○ Birds
   ○ Bricks

2. Mort puts out water for the _____ birds.

   ○ thirsty
   ○ third
   ○ think

3. Mort likes to hear the birds _____.

   ○ chip
   ○ shop
   ○ chirp

4. When a cat comes by, the birds _____ away!

- ○ slap
- ○ swim
- ○ swirl

5. They don't want the cat to _____ them.

- ○ hem
- ○ hurt
- ○ her

6. They _____ in a tree and wait for the cat to go away.

- ○ perch
- ○ peach
- ○ price

7. After a while, the cat _____ around and walks away.

- ○ tins
- ○ turns
- ○ trains

Go on

8. One bird family nested in a _____ tree.

○ fir
○ fix
○ fit

9. Mort waited and waited for the _____ egg to hatch.

○ fist
○ fur
○ first

10. By the _____ week, all the baby birds had hatched!

○ trick
○ third
○ thin

Name_____

r-Controlled Vowels: *ar*

Read each sentence. Then fill in the circle next to the word that makes sense in the sentence.

1. Mark and Fern live on a _____.

   ○ farm
   ○ firm
   ○ frame

2. They live quite _____ from town.

   ○ fur
   ○ fir
   ○ far

3. Their house is a _____ white farmhouse.

   ○ latch
   ○ large
   ○ leg

Go on

4. Near the house is a big red _____.

○ burn

○ brain

○ barn

5. Lots of animals are in the _____ by the barn.

○ yard

○ yam

○ corn

6. You can hear dogs _____, hens squawk, and pigs squeal.

○ bank

○ brick

○ bark

7. When it gets _____, Mark and Fern sit outside.

- ○ drink
- ○ dark
- ○ day

8. They look at all the _____ in the sky.

- ○ stacks
- ○ sirs
- ○ stars

9. Sometimes they catch fireflies in a _____.

- ○ jam
- ○ jar
- ○ jig

10. Life on a farm is fun, but it is also _____ work!

- ○ hard
- ○ hurt
- ○ had

STOP

Base Words and Endings *-er*, *-est*

Read each sentence. Then fill in the circle next to the word that makes sense in the sentence.

1. Jen ran _____ than anyone else today.

   ○ fastest
   ○ faster
   ○ fast

2. I kicked the ball the _____.

   ○ far
   ○ farther
   ○ farthest

3. Dad was _____ of everyone on the team.

   ○ proud
   ○ proudest
   ○ prouder

4. After the game, Jen and I were _____ than our dad!

○ hungrier
○ hungriest
○ hungry

5. We wanted the _____ hotdogs we could buy.

○ big
○ bigger
○ biggest

6. "These are the _____ hotdogs I've ever seen!" I said.

○ longer
○ longest
○ long

7. Then Dad said, "Do you want the _____ cone of all?"

○ larger
○ large
○ largest

Go on

8. We got _____ cones than Dad.

- ◯ smaller
- ◯ smallest
- ◯ small

9. But they were just as _____.

- ◯ colder
- ◯ cold
- ◯ coldest

10. I don't think anyone was _____ than we were.

- ◯ happier
- ◯ happy
- ◯ happiest

Name_____

High-Frequency Words

Read each sentence. Then fill in the circle next to the word that makes sense in the sentence.

1. We were playing _____ the best team in town.

   ○ against
   ○ divide
   ○ thoughts

2. It was only the third _____ of the game.

- ○ eyes
- ○ began
- ○ minute

3. The other team _____ had a home run.

- ○ head
- ○ present
- ○ already

4. Their player hit the ball, but I _____ it!

- ○ begin
- ○ caught
- ○ sure

5. It was our turn to bat, but would we be _____ to catch up?

- ○ break
- ○ able
- ○ above

STOP

 Name_____

Making Predictions

Read each part of the story. Then read each
question and fill in the circle next to the best
answer.

The Flute

Sue wanted to learn to play the flute. Her
mom had once played the flute. Sue's mom still
had the flute, but it was packed away
somewhere.

1. What do you think Sue will do next?

○ learn to play the drums

○ go to the store to buy a flute

○ ask if she can use her mother's flute

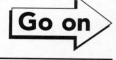

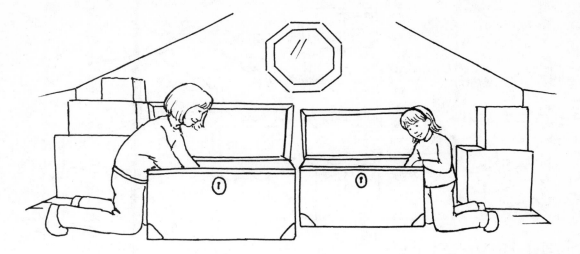

Sue and her mom looked everywhere, but they could not find the flute. "Maybe I gave it away," said Mom.

"Did you give it to Bob?" asked Sue. "He used to play the flute, too, didn't he?"

"He did," said Mom.

2. What do you think Sue and Mom will do?

- ○ drive away
- ○ call Bob
- ○ forget about the flute

3. What will they ask Bob?

- ○ if he has the flute
- ○ if he needs a new flute
- ○ if he broke the flute

Bob did have Mom's flute.

"Oh, good!" said Sue. "May I please use it?"

"I can even show you how to play it," said Bob. "But you'll have to come here so I can teach you. Maybe your mom can drive you."

4. What do you think Sue will do next?

- ○ ask Bob about his garden
- ○ ask Mom if she will drive her to Bob's
- ○ ask Mom about school

5. If there was more to this story, what do you think would happen?

- ○ Bob would teach Sue to play the flute.
- ○ Sue's mother would teach her to drive.
- ○ Sue would learn to paint with water colors.

G Name_____

Sequence of Events

Read the selection. Then read each question. Fill
in the circle next to the best answer.

A New Kind of Pet

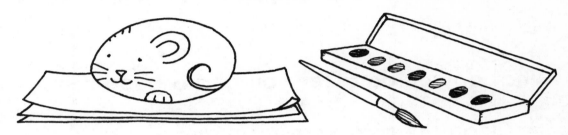

Here is how to make a pet rock.

First, find a round rock or a stone. Look for
one that's not too big. A rock about the size of
your hand will do.

Use soap and water to clean the rock. Then
let it dry. That may take some time.

When the rock is dry, get out your paints.
Choose the colors you want to use. Paint eyes, a
mouth, and a nose on the rock. Paint some fur,
too, if you wish.

Now put your pet to work. Your pet can hold
down papers. It can make your desk look nice.
Making a pet rock is fun!

Go on ⟹

1. If you want to make a pet rock, what is the first thing you do?

   ○ Draw a picture of your hand.
   ○ Get out your paints.
   ○ Find a round rock or stone.

2. What do you do after you find a good rock?

   ○ Clean the rock with soap and water.
   ○ Soak the rock in brown paint.
   ○ Make some fur for the pet.

3. What do you do after you wash the rock?

   ○ Put the pet rock to work.
   ○ Use soap and water to clean the rock.
   ○ Let the rock dry.

Go on

4. What do you do after the rock is dry?

- ○ Clean it again and again.
- ○ Paint a face on it.
- ○ Put it on your papers.

5. What do you do last?

- ○ Give the pet rock to your dog.
- ○ Put the pet rock on top of some papers.
- ○ Get out your paints.

Name_____

Cause and Effect

Read the selection. Then read each question.
Fill in the circle next to the best answer.

What a Good Dog!

If you have a dog, you need to train it. Big
dogs need to be trained, and so do small ones.

Many dogs like to jump up on people. Most
of the time, they are just being friendly. They
may want to give the person's face a lick. But a
big dog can knock a person over when it jumps.
A small dog with mud on its paws can get a
person dirty. That's why you need to teach
your dog not to jump up.

Go on ⇨

Dogs also need to know how to walk with people. Teach your dog not to pull you where it wants to go. Teach your dog to walk by your side. Teach it to stop when you stop.

1. Why shouldn't big dogs jump up on people?

- ○ Big dogs may knock people down.
- ○ Big dogs may be friendly.
- ○ Bigs dogs may walk with you.

2. Why shouldn't small dogs jump up on people?

- ○ The dogs may get sick.
- ○ The dogs may get a pet.
- ○ The dogs may get people dirty.

3. Why does a dog need to be trained to walk with you?

- ○ so it won't grow
- ○ so it won't pull you where it wants to go
- ○ so it can eat treats

You have to work hard
to train a dog. If your
dog does what you say,
give it a treat. Say, "Good
dog!" Then rub your dog's
chest and say it again.
Your dog will love it —
and people will love
your dog.

4. When would you give a dog treats?

○ when it jumps up on people
○ when it pulls on the leash
○ when it does what you say

**5. What else can you do so a dog will learn
from you?**

○ Yell at the dog.
○ Rub the dog's chest.
○ Let the dog jump up.

I

Name_____

Spelling

Read the sentence with the missing word. Find the right way to spell the word. Fill in the circle next to your answer.

1. The snow fell and the wind blew all _____.

   ○ mornin
   ○ morening
   ○ morning

2. When it stopped, Dad and I looked at

   our _____.

   ○ yerd
   ○ yad
   ○ yard

3. It was still very cold, so I wore my _____ coat.

   ○ warmist
   ○ warmest
   ○ wormest

4. The snow was _____ near the porch.

   ○ depst
   ○ depest
   ○ deepest

5. "So where shall we _____ to dig?" Dad asked.

   ○ start
   ○ star
   ○ stirt

J Name_____

Grammar

Read each sentence. Then fill in the circle next to the word that makes sense in the sentence.

1. "This peach smells _____," said Gail.

    ○ fresh
    ○ hard
    ○ soft

2. "Feel the skin," said Rob.
    "It's so _____!"

    ○ fishy
    ○ loud
    ○ fuzzy

3. "Let's get some!" said Gail. "I bet they
    taste _____."

    ○ sweet
    ○ mad
    ○ smooth

4. Dad picked out the _____ pie he
could find.

- ○ big
- ○ bigger
- ○ biggest

5. Then Mom said, "Look! This pie is
even _____ than yours!"

- ○ thick
- ○ thicker
- ○ thickest

STOP

Name_____

Writing Skills

Look at each picture, and read the sentences that tell about it. Fill in the circle next to the sentence that describes the picture most clearly.

1. ○ Nan got a puppy.
   ○ Nan's new puppy is cute.
   ○ Nan's little puppy has dark fur and a coal-black nose.

2. ○ Jon thinks cats make the best pets.
   ○ Jon's cat has long, silky fur.
   ○ Jon's pet is a cat.

3. ○ Meg keeps her fish in a bowl.
   ○ Meg's fish has black stripes and large fins.
   ○ Meg's fish is mostly black.

Go on

4. ○ Tim has two white mice with dark eyes and long tails.
   ○ I would not want to have a mouse for a pet.
   ○ Tim likes to play with his pet mice.

5. ○ My dog has toys to play with.
   ○ My dog has a green toy frog that makes loud squeaks.
   ○ Not all frogs are green.